Facilitator's
for the Class of No
by Susan Ives

MW01071294

Susan has been on the core team of the San Antonio peaceCENTER since 1998.
A native of Bucks County, PA, Susan has a degree in political science
from Drew University in Madison NJ
and is a former army officer and Gulf War veteran.
You can reach her at suives@texas.net.

Additional copies of this manual
and other peaceCENTER BOOKS
can be ordered from
www.salsa.net/peace/ebooks

The modest amount we charge for these books
funds the work of the peaceCENTER

**Focused on the vision of God's peace, the peaceCENTER supports the learning
of peace in our lives and the demonstration of peace within our community**

**peaceCENTER
1443 S. St. Mary's
San Antonio, TX 78210
210-224-HOPE
www.salsa.net/peace**

Preface

The San Antonio peaceCENTER has been facilitating Colman McCarthy's *Class of Nonviolence* for more than a decade, offering one or two sessions a year in venues as diverse as university classrooms and local pizza joints. We've had groups as small as five and as large as thirty. The participants have ranged from committed elders in the peace movement to skeptical students.

If you are looking for more insight into teaching *The Class of Nonviolence*, please read Colman McCarthy's "**I'd Rather Teach Peace**" (Orbis Books, April 2002.) Colman, a former board member of the peaceCENTER and the director of the Center for Teaching Peace in Washington, D.C., designed this curriculum and has taught it to more than 7,000 students in high schools, universities and prisons. He's the man.

The emphasis of *this* manual is on exercises that complement the reading material: film clips, art, reflections, games, poetry, simulations and the like. These exercises are optional: the entire class time can be spent in a facilitated discussion of the readings and sometimes that's exactly what we do.

There are times, however, when we want to experience the material in a different way than reading-and-talking, to move it from our heads to our hearts. We like to nudge words and jiggle ideas, to see and touch and hear and taste and smell peace.

We call our way of learning "experiential." The emphasis is on the lifetime of experience that the participants bring to the class. Their experiences inform the readings. The readings illuminate their experience. The exercises open everyone to the process. The great wonder of this class is that every session is different. We may have facilitated it many, many times but each time we come to it with beginner's minds, as the experiences of *these* students, the insights of *today's* lesson, the interaction among *this* group of people at *this* moment make the words fresh, as if we were encountering them for the first time.

Although my name appears as the author of this manual it is, of course, based on the collective wisdom of everyone who has been through this class with me, especially the other members of the peaceCENTER Core Team: as I write this, Ann Helmke, Rosalyn Collier, Barbie Gorelick, Narjis Pierre, Maureen Leach, Rebecca Matavele and Alyssa Burgin. All the good stuff is theirs.

Susan Ives, San Antonio, Texas   August 9, 2007

On August 9, the first Indian reservation, Brotherton, was established in New Jersey. (1758) Franz Jagerstatter, an Austrian conscientious objector who refused to serve in the army of the Third Reich, was publicly beheaded in Berlin. (1943) The second atomic bomb, Fatman, was dropped on the arms-manufacturing and key port city of Nagasaki. (1945) 20,000 women demonstrated against the pass laws in Pretoria, South Africa. (1956) Two hundred people staged a sit-in at the New York City offices of Dow Chemical to protest use of napalm in Vietnam. (1966)

Foreword
by Colman McCarthy

I f it's true that all governments say they want peace and if it's true that all human hearts yearn for peace, a question arises: why isn't peace education given a place in our lives, whether our academic lives, our political lives or our spiritual lives?

Susan Ives is in the front ranks of peace educators who are answering that question by making available the literature of peace in a form that is both creative and practical. Her "Facilitator's Manual" is a book guaranteed to open minds, uplift spirits and inspire action. Her diligence brings to mind the memorable line of Eleanor Roosevelt: "*Some people are dreamers and some people are doers, but what the world really needs are dreamers who do and doers who dream.*"

"Facilitator's Manual" appears at a moment when peace education is seeing signs of success. Nationally, more than 300 colleges and universities are offering majors or minors in peace studies. Graduates schools such as American University in Washington, the University of Notre Dame and the University of San Diego are flooded with applications. The Rotary World Peace Fellowship annually provides some 60 students with all-expenses paid grants in a master's degree program at selected universities. High school and elementary schools are increasingly adding courses in peace studies and conflict resolution.

My own involvement began in 1982 when I volunteered to teach a course on nonviolence at a Washington D.C. high school not far from my office at the Washington Post. The students were able to grasp intellectually what they already absorbed emotionally: the haunting awareness that their future is threatened and their present swamped by military, family, verbal, institutional and environmental violence. The course went well, with plenty of time for debate and discussion. Soon after, I took the course to Georgetown University Law Center, American University, the University of Maryland and two more high schools. In 25 years, I've had more than 7,000 students in my courses. As a lifelong pacifist, I've had my hunches confirmed. Yes, peacemaking can be taught, the literature is large and growing. Yes, our schools should be offering academic courses on alternatives to violence. Yes, parents and teachers are realizing that unless we teach our children peace, someone else will teach them violence.

Based on those positives, my wife and I in the mid-1980s founded the Center for Teaching Peace, a non-profit that helps schools to get courses on peace studies into the nation's 78,000 elementary schools, 32,000 high schools and 3,100 colleges and universities. We operate on the belief that it is easier to build a peaceful child than repair a violent adult.

I'm both grateful and honored that Susan Ives has taken the readings from my text, "The Class of Nonviolence," and bolstered them with the richness of meaningful exercises that range from films to classroom simulations. With her "Facilitator's Manual," Susan Ives has created a work of art. But a work of art is first of all work.

As you read through these pages, I am betting that you will be energized by the author's efforts to work hard—and then either begin or expand your commitment to peacemaking, whether across the ocean or across the living room.

Washington, D.C.   August, 2007

Table of Contents

"A conclusion is simply the place
where someone got tired of thinking."
Arthur Block

Getting Started

You can do it!

I initially hesitated to write this manual because I was concerned that I was making it too hard. At the peaceCENTER we call it *bringing in the circus elephants*, that dysfunctional tendency to take something that is wonderfully simple and adding a little of this and throwing in a bit of that until it turns into something COMPLICATED. Simple is good. Complicated is bad.

This class *is* simple. Read, reflect, converse. That's all.

When we have interns at the peaceCENTER the first thing we often ask them to do is facilitate a class of nonviolence. Get a group together (two is a group.) Read the essays. Talk about them. That's it. You don't have to be an "expert" on nonviolence. You don't have to be trained as a teacher or be an experienced public speaker. You don't have to have a college degree. You don't have to be legally an adult, part of an organization or have shared a jail cell with Martin Luther King, Jr.. You just have to be *you*, welcoming and open enough to let the class be what it wants and needs to be.

Read, reflect, converse. Really: that's it!

However, here at the peaceCENTER we have facilitated this class many times and have noticed that some people get antsy if they can't move around a little. Some crave visual stimulation or become impatient with the abstract intellectualism of much of the material. Sometimes every-one just runs out of steam. These exercises are techniques we have used to augment — not replace — reading, reflecting and conversing.

These are not rigid lesson plans. Take what you need and leave the rest. If you tried to cram in every exercise you would spend a full day on every lesson (we generally allocate about two hours.) If you want to change something, change it. If you want to shuffle an exercise to a different lesson, go right ahead. If you want to replace our stories with your own — so much the better.

Distributing the Materials

The 48 essays that comprise student readings for the Class of Nonviolence are available for free online at **<www.salsa.net/peace/conv>**.

Some people may not be able to get online to download the class materials.

> You can have people call you before the first class session and make arrangements to get the materials to them.

> You can have a few extra copies on loan for the duration of the class.

You can download the class materials as a MS Word file onto CDs for the students to take to a local copy shop for reproduction at their own expense. This can be helpful to people with poor eyesight: the copy shop can expand the type size to a bigger font that is easier to read.

You can take orders and reproduce the materials yourself for distribution at the next class session. These cost us about $6, and we ask for a donation to cover our out-of-pocket expenses.

Weaving the sessions together

When we advertise the class we invite people to attend one session or the entire series, recognizing that eight weeks is an impossible commitment for many. However, the whole of this class is much bigger than the sum of its parts, so we take every opportunity to reinforce that each lesson builds on the one before it. In addition to having an opening and closing ritual (pages 9-10), we have found that these activities emphasize the connection of each part to the whole:

Display/Altar: For each lesson we create a small display, or, if you feel comfortable with the concept, an altar, and add to it as the class progresses. There are suggestions of what to include in your display to provide a focal point for that day's learning.

This Day in History: Every day of the year we have an opportunity to celebrate an event in peace and justice history. There is a list on the peaceCENTER's Web site, at <www.salsa.net/peace/timeline/index.html>. It adds a sense of immediacy and importance to a lesson to briefly recall that yesterday was Gandhi's birthday or that next week is the anniversary of the first Greensboro lunch counter sit-in.

Review of previous lesson
Some people think quickly on their feet but others prefer to mull things over the course of a few days. At the beginning of every session we ask if anyone had any new insights (or questions) about previous discussions. Keep this short – 5 or 10 minutes at the most – so you have time to cover the new material.

Journaling
Many of the participants in our classes of nonviolence have journaled and shared some of their entries with the class. We don't require journaling but the process of reading-reflecting-writing activates a different part of the brain than reading-reflecting-talking. We recommend it as a way for the students to go deeper into the material and invite the participants to share if they choose to do so.

End of lesson evaluation
At the end of each lesson it can be helpful to take a minute to ask: what worked well for you today? What didn't work as well?

Beginning and ending

We honor everyone's other commitments by starting and ending on time. We arrive early enough to have everything set up (audio-visuals tested, art supplies laid out) and are thus centered and welcoming when people show up.

One way to signify the beginning and end of your formal time together is with a short ritual: perhaps quiet centering at the beginning of each session and a formal gathering at the end. There are several examples on pages 9-10.

Class Set-up

If at all possible, seat everyone in a circle, a semicircle or around a table. This emphasizes that learning is collaborative and facilitates active listening: it's hard to be fully engaged when you are staring at the back of someone's head.

Guest speakers

"Experts" tend to change the dynamic of the class from one of open and active exploration to one of passive knowledge acquisition. We break our own rule by inviting our local Catholic Workers to the session on Dorothy Day: they've been through the class themselves and understand how it works. Otherwise, you have all the expertise you need right in your group.

Share the work

You don't have to do this all yourself. Many times we share the facilitation: divvy it up among the class members at the first session. If you have a display/altar, let someone else be in charge of creating it. Have someone else handle the evaluation, or the opening meditation. If supplies are needed, ask for volunteers to collect and bring them. Someone might want to provide snacks, set out ice water or rearrange tables and chairs.

Neither right nor left

The class is neither right nor left, conservative nor liberal, Democrat nor Republican. This is not to say that the class is not political: it is deeply political in the sense of "politics" being the "work of the people." It is most emphatically not, however, partisan. The conversation will, however, inevitably veer towards partisan issues. It is the job of the facilitator to remain neutral, to maintain civility and to ensure that those in the minority are not bullied into silence.

Activism

As the class learns more about nonviolence some of the participants may want to DO something. Although it is our most fervent wish that this class will lead to action, be sensitive about incorporating action into the body of the class. This is an *exploratory* journey and not everyone will be ready to commit, or to commit to a particular cause. Some will be uncomfortable if they feel pressured to do so.

We will invite people to act ("there's a death penalty vigil Monday night at 6 – you're welcome to come" or "we're circulating a petition about landmines in the back of the room; feel free to take a stack with you.") We invite others in the class to do the same. However, it's not fair for the facilitator to make the action a required part of the class, to put people on the spot. If the class, by consensus, decides to act, fine, as long as no one is pressured. That's not fair.

This is not the only class

We've noticed a tendency in ourselves to treat this as THE class of nonviolence — the only one anyone will ever have to attend. We've tried to cram everything in that anyone will ever need. It doesn't work.

This is a beginner's class that concentrates on reading and discussing primary documents about the history and philosophy of nonviolence. That is its strength. It is not a comprehensive class on the civil rights movement, or hands-on training in preparation for a direct action, or a leadership institute for organizers, or a seminar to bring you up to speed on current issues. Let this class be what it wants to be. It's a great class that can lead to more classes, on other topics, with a different slant. It's the beginning — not the end.

Things change

There are a lot of Web references in this manual. They may change, or disappear. If addresses change, or if we have to correct an error we will post changes on the peaceCENTER Web site, at <www.salsa.net/peace/ebooks/fmconv.html>. If you find errors, please send them to suives@texas.net.

Visit our blog!

We now have a blog at <classofnonviolence.blogspot.com>. We're keeping it current with new resources that we discover.

We'd love to hear from you

If you host a class of Nonviolence, with or without the assistance of this manual, let us know — it gladdens our hearts to know that this material is being used. Send an e-mail to suives@texas.net or call the peaceCENTER at 210-224-HOPE.

Opening Reflection: Quiet Centering

Rosalyn, in particular, likes to start each session with a short meditation to collect ourselves individually and as a group to deepen the transformative potential of the class. Here's an example of a five-minute guided meditation:

Clearly and calmly begin with the following words:

"Begin by putting aside anything on your lap or in your hands. *(pause)*
Place your feet flat on the floor and rest your hands in your lap. *(pause)*
Allow the chair to support the weight of your body, settle in. *(pause)*
Close your eyes. *(pause)*

Inhale slowly through your nose and exhale slowly through your mouth.
As you inhale, straighten your spine, drop your shoulders. *(pause)*

Begin exhaling, blowing out through your mouth any thought or concern which keeps you from being fully present here today. *(pause)*

Inhale, bringing your head up over your body, not leaning forward.
Imagine your breath filling your entire body, not stopping at your chest.

As you exhale, gently drop your left ear down to your left shoulder, feeling the s...l...o...w... stretch in your right neck muscles.

Inhale, bringing your head back upright to center.

Exhale deliberately dropping your right ear down to your right shoulder,
feel the relaxing release of tension from your left neck muscles.

Slowly inhale, bringing yourself, your head back to center. Briefly hold this breath. *(pause)*

This time as you blow out through your mouth, carefully lower your chin
to your chest, feeling your back loosen up. *(pause)*

Inhale, bringing yourself back to center. *(pause)*

Placing your right hand over your heart, continue the slow deliberate
breathing for a few minutes, opening yourself to this strong center."

(continue the silent breathing for an additional three minutes.)

Closing Ritual: The Pledge of Nonviolence

The Pledge of Nonviolence was developed by the United Nations. For more information about the U.N. Decade for a Culture of Peace and Nonviolence, visit <www.unesco.org/manifesto2000>. One way to end each session is to have everyone stand in a circle and recite this pledge. Either furnish each person with a copy or write it on big paper and tack it to the wall.

Peace is in Our Hands

I pledge
In my daily life
In my family
My work
My community
My country
and my region to:
Listen to understand
Share with others
Preserve the planet
Rediscover solidarity
Reject violence
Respect all life

Closing Ritual: Prayer of St. Francis

This Christian prayer can be adapted in an interfaith or secular setting by eliminating the words in brackets. This is an excellent definition of peace with justice and, like the United Nations Pledge, empowers each person to be an agent of change.

[Lord,]
make me an instrument of [Thy] peace;
where there is hatred, let me sow love;
where there is injury, pardon;
where there is doubt, faith;
where there is despair, hope;
where there is darkness, light;
and where there is sadness, joy.

[O Divine Master,]
grant that I may not so much
seek to be consoled as to console;
to be understood, as to understand;
to be loved, as to love;
for it is in giving that we receive,
it is in pardoning that we are pardoned,
[and it is in dying that we are born to Eternal Life.]
[Amen]

Communicating Nonviolence: Be the Change

Gandhi advised that we "Be the Change we wish to see in the world." With this always in mind, we model these community conversations in such a way that the students have opportunities to increase their confidence to discuss difficult and controversial issues deeply, compassionately and with an open mind. We start with a discussion of reflective listening and use communications exercises if and when they are needed.

Your role as group leader is to help group members teach themselves: to facilitate sharing what they know and contributing to everyone's understanding. Make it clear that learning is a shared responsibility and for this process to succeed everyone should have done the reading, thought about it, considered any questions that have occurred to them and participate in the discussion.

Competitive or Combative Listening happens when we are more interested in promoting our own point of view than in understanding or exploring someone else's view. We either listen for openings to take the floor, or for flaws or weak points we can attack. As we pretend to pay attention we are impatiently waiting for an opening, or internally formulating our rebuttal and planning our devastating comeback that will destroy their argument and make us the victor.

Active or Reflective Listening happens when we are genuinely interested in understanding what the other person is thinking, feeling, wanting or what the message means, and we are active in checking out our understanding before we respond with our own new message. We restate or paraphrase our understanding of their message and reflect it back to the sender for verification.

We invite the class to agree on how the class works together. If you want, you can post your agreements on the wall, review them at the start of every session and revise them as the need arises. Some suggestions:

> Speak one at a time
> Listen actively, without judgment
> Be critical of ideas, not people
> Stick to the subject
> Dialogue, not debate
> Share experiences instead of giving advice
> Acknowledge that we all hold a piece of the truth
> Invite a moment of silence if tensions arise
> Ensure confidentiality if requested

Communications Exercise: Deep Listening

Time: 10 -15 minutes
Supplies: none

Have the class pair off. Have one person in each pair volunteer to be "A" and the other "B." Explain that the "A" person is going to talk for three minutes and that the "B" person is going to listen intently, without saying anything but trying to convey with their entire body that they are attentive and listening deeply.

You can either have the participants talk about anything of their choosing or provide them with a question to answer. Some suggestions:
If I suddenly found out that I had 24 hours to live I would spend them . . . . .
If I had to give up some modern convenience, like TV, car, toilet, telephone, lighting, I would select . . . .

At the end of the three minutes, call for a minute of reflective silence. Then, ask the As what it felt like to be listened to with total attention. Then, ask the Bs what it felt like to listen with total attention.

When that discussion is complete, switch roles and ask the Bs to talk and the As to listen. You can use the same question or a different one. After three minutes of talking/listening and another minute of reflective silence, ask again what it felt like to talk and to listen. Also, ask if their prior experience as a talker or a listener changed the way they behaved or the way they felt.

Communications Exercise: Mustard Tastes Like . . .

Time: about 5 minutes
Supplies: pretzel sticks, a jar of mustard

Thanks to Marietta McCarty and her book "*Little Big Minds: Sharing Philosophy with Kids*" (Tarcher/Penguin, 2006) for this exercise.

Put out a bag of small pretzel sticks and a jar of mustard. Ask each person to dip a pretzel into the mustard, taste it, then describe the taste of the mustard in one word. Bitter. Spicy. Tangy.

After everyone has tasted and described the taste, explain (if they haven't figured it out for themselves) that each of us brings a different physiology, different tastes and different experiences to the table. No response is wrong, no response is right for the whole group. We have to figure it out for ourselves and although we may not always agree, we all taste the mustard.

"The sad truth is that most evil is done by people who never make up their minds to be good or evil."

Hannah Arendt

Class of Nonviolence
Lesson 1
Introduction to Nonviolence

Essays for Lesson One

If We Listen Well by Edward Guinan
Nonviolent Response to Assault by Gerald Vanderhaar
Human Nature Isn't Inherently Violent by Alfie Kohn
Axioms of Nonviolence By Lanza del Vasto
Teaching Reverence for Life by Albert Schweitzer
Students Astutely Aware by Colman McCarthy

Questions for Lesson One

Explain what you think nonviolence means.

Peter Maurin wrote that "society should be so structured that it is easy for people to be good." Do you think this is an idle dream? If achievable, would it make us more peaceful in our relationships?

Many anthropologists point to the violence in the animal kingdom as evidence that human animals are prone innately to violence. Are we really inherently violent or have we "learned" violence from others, from society?

Of all the forms of violence — physical, verbal, psychological, spiritual — which have you experienced and how did it impact you?

Can a nonviolent lifestyle be attained easily in the face of a government which resorts to violence to resolve its conflicts;
is there a carryover effect from top-to-bottom stemming from
a powerful example from one's own national government?

During the first session we start to build our community of peacemakers: get to know each other, share our hopes, expectations and fears and learn how to talk to each other about difficult issues. We start defining nonviolence.

Start, if you feel comfortable doing so, with a few minutes of silence or a guided meditation.

If the group doesn't know each other well, spend a few minutes on brief introductions, perhaps asking what brought each person to this class and what they hope to get out of it. You might want to conduct a more structured icebreaker (we've provided a few on the following pages) or use one that has worked for you in the past.

Don't forget to pass around a sign-up sheet. You should be able to contact people if a class is cancelled because of inclement weather or if there is a change of venue. If it's a large group you may want to provide nametags.

The display or altar for this day can be simple, as you will be adding to it in future sessions. Perhaps include some of the words and phrases used in the essays: peace, nonviolence, reverence for life, human nature, truth, love, satyagraha, justice, etc. You can copy a few of the quotations from <www.salsa.net/peace/quotes.html>. A candle. Always a candle.

At the first class not everyone will have figured out how to access the materials and may not have read the essays. Fortunately, the five questions that Colman McCarthy suggests for this session can generate a lively and fruitful discussion independent of the readings. Those who have done their homework will add depth to the conversation and provide a model for future sessions.

Who are the authors in this session?

Edward Guinan: former Paulist priest, founder of the Community for Creative Nonviolence <users.erols.com/ccnv/> in Washington, D.C.

Gerald Vanderhaar: Professor Emeritus of Religion and Peace studies at Christian Brothers University in Memphis and Pax Christi - USA Ambassador of Peace

Alfie Kohn: writes and speaks widely on human behavior, education, and parenting <www.alfiekohn.org>.

Lanza del Vasto: a Christian disciple of Gandhi, founded in the forties The Ark (*Communautés de l'Arche*) in France. Gandhi gave him the name *Shantidas*, "Servant of Peace".

Albert Schweitzer: an Alsatian theologian, musician, philosopher, and physician. He received the 1952 Nobel Peace Prize for his philosophy of "reverence for life."

Ice Breaker: The Network of Mutuality

> **"Injustice anywhere is a threat to justice everywhere. We are caught in an inescapable network of mutuality, tied in a single garment of destiny."** *Martin Luther King*

Time: 5-10 minutes, depending on the size of the group
Supplies: A big ball of string or a hank of yarn

Have everyone stand in a circle. The leader holds a ball of string or yarn. Explain that we are going to create a "network of mutuality," as described by Dr. King. Read the quotation.

The leader explains that we are going to begin getting to know each other. Start by modeling a short statement about yourself: "My name is Susan, I work at the peaceCENTER and I'm really excited about learning from each one of you as we explore nonviolence."

Then, hold onto the end of the string and explain that you are going to toss the ball to someone across the circle who will then introduce his or herself. Make sure to make a clear signal, have eye contact or call out the person's name so they know its coming! After they catch the ball and make their introduction, explain that they are to hold onto the string and toss the ball to another person. Keep it going until everyone has a chance to participate (in a small group you might toss it around two or three times.)

When you are done, ask people to look at the web they have made and ask them to reflect on it. What does it say to you? You can read the quotation from Martin Luther King again. Here's another quotation that applies:

> **"In the final analysis, our most basic common link is that we all inhabit this small planet; we all breathe the same air; we all cherish our children's future; and we all are mortal."** *John Fitzgerald Kennedy*

Leave a few moments of silence, and then (if there is enough space) carefully place the Web on the floor and leave it there during your class session.

As people make their way back to their seats you can, if you want, play a song. A perfect complement that reflects the web you have just made is "*The Great Mandala*," available on Peter Paul and Mary's "Songs of Conscience and Concern." Another is "*I Be Your Water*", on Sweet Honey in the Rock "In This Land." Or, try Freebo's "*We are All One People*," on "Peace is Our Birthright," available from <www.songsofpeace.org>.

Icebreaker: My New Best Friend

Time: 10-20 minutes, depending on the size of the group
Supplies: none, although the students may want scratch paper and a pen

Ask everyone to pair up with someone they do not know, or do not know well. Give them five minutes to interview each other, telling them that they will be responsible for introducing their partner. It can add depth to their interview if you ask them to discover at least one thing they have in common and at least one difference. At the end of five minutes, go around the circle and ask each person to introduce his or her partner to the group. If the group is large, instead of introducing everyone to everyone, have them break into smaller groups of 4, 6 or 8 people and perform the introductions within that group. If it is a group where everyone knows each other well, you can ask them to find out one new or surprising thing about the person they are interviewing and introducing.

Icebreaker: Call me by My Name

Time: about a minute or two per participant
Supplies: None

Ask each person to tell the group something special about their name. It might be a story about the aunt she was named after, an immigration official who bungled his surname at Ellis Island several generations ago, how she got an unusual nickname or how nobody can pronounce his name. The stories are funny, moving and, above all, memorable.

Creativity Exercise: Wrestling with Nonviolence

Time: about 5 minutes
Purpose: To encourage creative thinking about nonviolent alternatives
Supplies: Watch or clock with a second hand; tables.

This exercise and variations of it are used in nonviolence training all over the world.

Pair people up and tell them they are going to arm wrestle. The winners in this game are the ones who move their opponent's arm to the table four times in 30 seconds. (If you have a lot of people you can have two wrestlers and a scorer in each group, which is also a way to accommodate people who may be too fragile for arm wrestling.) Make sure they understand the rules: 30 seconds, four times. After everyone has arranged themselves give the 5-4-3-2-1 countdown and say GO! Keep an eye on what everyone is doing.

Most groups will play his as a win-lose game: they will try hard to defeat their opponents. Sometimes you will have a group that "sees through" this exercise and has two winners – ask them how they managed it. If not, ask the group to recall the rules. Then, ask them to figure out if there is a way that everyone can win – a win-win solution. (It's by cooperating – 1-2-3-4 down for me 1-2-3-4 down for you and we both win by getting four downs in the allotted 30 seconds. There may be other, equally valid solutions.)

Start a short discussion about the message of this exercise. Some of the answers you might get are:
> * We get used to doing things one way (playing to win) so we never explore if there is a better way
> * If we take the time to talk to each other we can finds ways where we both win.

> In this first session it can be helpful to read one of the essays out loud to stress the importance of the readings and to provide everyone with a common basis for discussion. The first one, "*If We Listen Well*," by Edward Guinan, lends itself to this. The leader can start by reading the first paragraph or two and then suggest that someone else take over until they are ready to pass it on. By sharing the reading you emphasize that this class is collaboration rather than a solo performance.

Films for this session

We generally do not include a film during the first session. However, if you have a convenient video setup a GREAT selection is *Nobelity*: *a look at the future through the eyes of nine Nobel laureates*. You can get it at <www.nobelity.org>. Although the film is 84 minutes long, each interview lasts only about five minutes and is conveniently positioned at the beginning of a scene. We recommend showing up to four interviews from the Peace Prize laureates: use one five-minute interview to introduce each one of the readings.

> **Jody Williams** from the International Campaign to Ban Land Mines talks about change and the power of one person to change the world
>
> **Sir Joseph Rotblatt** talks about peace and the threat of nuclear weapons
>
> **Archbishop Desmond Tutu** talks about love and forgiveness and the human capacity to do great things.
>
> **Wangaari Maathai** talks about persistence and the connection between the environment and peace. (this clip also works well with session 8, as do the first two clips on the DVD, which are about global warming and energy consumption.)

Reflective Exercise: Defining Nonviolence

Time: about 15-20 minutes
Supplies: copy of the definitions for each student (next page); writing implements

Give each person a copy of these three definitions. Have someone slowly read each definition. At the end of each definition, ask the students to reflect on the definition and to underline the words or phrases that are most meaningful. After a few minutes of reflection, discuss these insights as a group. Is there anything you would like to change in these definitions? If so, what and why? Move onto the next definition.

What is peace?

Peace is not the absence of violence or conflict but the presence of compassionate, all-inclusive love that engages the world and relationships.

What is violence?

Violence is emotional, verbal or physical behavior that dominates diminishes or destroys ourselves or others. Violence crosses boundaries without permission, disrupts authentic relationships and separates us from other beings.

(Definition adapted from: From Violence to Wholeness, Ken Butigan, Pace e Bene Franciscan Nonviolence Center, 1999)

What is nonviolence?

For many, nonviolence is a way of life that is grounded in a deeply held moral conviction. For others, it is a strategy, a method of confronting conflict or oppression in a way that seeks to honor life. Nonviolence:

- •is a kind of persistent, disciplined, assertive and often courageous good will,
- •Is active confrontation with evil that respects the personhood of an enemy,
- •seeks both to end the oppression or threat of violence and to reconcile the adversary.

(Adapted from the Evangelical Lutheran Church in America (ELCA) Task Force for the Decade of a Culture of Peace and Nonviolence)

Exercise: Nonviolence Grid

Time: Half hour, plus time to process and de-brief
Supplies: Cardstock to mark the four quadrants

The Nonviolence Grid is a technique used by the Fellowship of Reconciliation in the Peacemaker Training Institute to explore feelings toward various social issues while physically moving throughout the room, experiencing opinions in spatial proximity to each other.

Place four large cards on the ground. The North and East cards have large "plus" symbols, and the West and South cards have "minus" symbols on them. The North/South axis represents "better for society" and "worse for society" and the East/West axis represents "more violent" and "less violent". Make enough room to move around. At the start of the game the students all bunch in the middle of the room.

```
            + Better for society
   ┌─────────────────┬──────────────────┐
   │                 │                  │
 + │                 │                  │ -
 M │                 │                  │ L
 o │                 │                  │ e
 r │─────────────────○──────────────────│ s
 e │                 │                  │ s
   │                 │                  │
 v │                 │                  │ v
 i │                 │                  │ i
 o │                 │                  │ o
 l │                 │                  │ l
 e │                 │                  │ e
 n │                 │                  │ n
 t │                 │                  │ t
   └─────────────────┴──────────────────┘
            - Worse for society
```
Floor set-up

The leader reads the following opinion statements and then asks students to move in the room to the place on the grid which best fits their feelings toward the statement. For example: "If a storefront is vandalized, is it better or worse for society, more or less violent?" (If this is too complicated for your group, start with just the violent nonviolent axis and add the second dimension as they get more familiar with the process.)

The students then move to their places on the grid. The leader asks various students to explain why they are standing where they are. The leader may spend between 3-5 minutes on each question, and students can move if they change their minds.

The following questions are samples; feel free to invent your own:

Is it more or less violent, better or worse for society
to spank a 4-year-old who is misbehaving?
to arm airline pilots?
to attack someone before they have the chance to attack you?
to execute convicted killers?
to break into a lab and free chimpanzees that are being abused for
     medical experiments?

After the exercise is complete, these questions will help everyone process the experience: How did you feel about having other people know literally where you stand on different issues? How did it feel to see that everyone did not agree on the answers? What do you think this game represents in a larger society? Should everyone agree on the answers to these questions? What was difficult about this game? What did you learn about yourself in this game? What did you learn about your classmates in this game?

Exercise: Nonviolent Response to Assault

Time: 15-20 minutes

Supplies: three copies of the "three events" in the second essay, "*Nonviolent Response to Assault*," by Gerard A. Vanderhaar

Break the class into three groups. Have each group discuss one of the events for five-ten minutes (keep an eye on the groups to monitor when the conversation begins to flag.) Have each group present their insights, and give everyone the opportunity to reflect on the ideas that arise. During the first session, when not everyone may have read the essays, this is an effective way to notch up the quality of the discussion.

Reflection: Fight, Flight and Nonviolence

Time: 10 minutes

Supplies: None

"Nonviolence" is an awkward word: we wish there was a better one, or that we lived in a world that had never conceived of a word for violence but instead had to clumsily refer to it as "non-peace" or "non-safety." Nonviolence sounds like it is simply the opposite of violence, which is often taken to mean passivity, weakness or avoidance. We often refer to "creative nonviolence," "active nonviolence" or "nonviolent resistance" to emphasize that nonviolence is neither fight (violence) nor flight (passivity) but rather a unique third way of engaging and transforming conflict.

An example we often recount is one described by Walter Wink in his book "*Violence and Nonviolence in South Africa: Jesus' Third Way*." Tell this story interactively to help everyone refine their definition of nonviolence.

A black woman was walking on a South African street with her children, when a white man, passing, spat in her face.

Ask the class, how might she have responded with violence? (some responses might be that she could have spit back at him, cursed at him or hit him.) And what might the result of such a response have been? (He could have had her arrested, beat her up, or even killed her.)

What could her possible passive responses have been? (she could have just hung her head and walked on.) And what might the result have been? (she could have felt humiliated, or angry; her children could have learned that white men can spit on them without consequences.)

So what did this woman do? Wink reported that she stopped and said, "Thank you, and now for the children," moving them to the front so that he could spit on them, too. The man was put off balance and was unable to respond. We hope he took the opportunity to reflect that he had become a monster who spits on women and children and changed his ways. This is the transformative potential of nonviolence: it lifts the veil that hides the violence and opens the possibility of healing. (In ancient Greek, the root word for *Apocalypse* meant "the lifting of the veil," or the revelation of something that was hidden.)

The black woman on the sidewalk perfectly demonstrated what Jesus described to his followers as "turning the other cheek." This, too, is often interpreted as passivity: hit me again! On the contrary, turning the other cheek is a creative and courageous act of nonviolence. It is saying: "you hit me once and it may have stung my flesh but it did not and cannot touch my dignity as a human being. Your violence did not work. Now, if you want, do it again, but this time look me in the eye, equal-to-equal, fully conscious of what you are doing, of who you are and who I am."

Nonviolence — this "third way" alternative to fight or flight — is a way of turning the world's power relationships upside-down. It is subversion at the deepest level. To us, this is the most important lesson in the entire class.

Exercise: Perpetrator, Bystander, Victim, Healer
Time: 15 minutes
Supplies: Pencil, paper

This exercise helps people confront their own complex relationship with violence. It helps answer one of Colman McCarthy's questions for this session: "*Of all the forms of violence — physical, verbal, psychological, spiritual — which have you experienced and how did it impact you?*" It should be done towards the end of this session when everyone has a solid understanding of all of the terms.

Have everyone draw a four-box grid on their piece of paper, labeling them: fight, flight, victim, healer. Assure everyone that no one will have to share their grid if they don't choose to: acknowledging our own violence or our own victimhood can be personal and painful.

Ask everyone to spend a moment in quiet reflection and to recall a time when they:
1. Were a perpetrator of violence (fight)
2. Were a bystander to violence (flight)
3. Were a victim of violence (victim)
4. Acted nonviolently (healer)

Give everyone about five minutes to quietly reflect and to add items to the grid. Afterwards, ask if anyone want to share any of their entries, or comment on their feelings about the process.

"I think a pillow should be the peace symbol, not the dove. The pillow has more feathers than the dove, and it doesn't have a beak to peck you with." Jack Handey

Art project: Peace Symbols

Time: 20-25 minutes
Supplies: Paper, crayons or markers; Dictionary of Peace Symbols (next page)

Introduce the concept of peace symbols and briefly describe the meaning of various symbols listed in the peaceCENTER's dictionary of peace symbols (you might make a copy and post it on the wall for reference or even make a copy for each group.) Read the quotation about the pillow. Divide into groups of two or three. Ask each group to design a peace symbol of their own. After about 10 minutes, ask each group to explain their symbol to the group.

Reflective Exercise: A letter to myself

Time: About 15 minutes
Supplies: envelopes, paper, pens or pencils

At the beginning of the session, place the supplies in a central location. Explain that at the end of this session everyone will have the opportunity to write a letter to his or her self, and that you will hold onto the sealed envelopes and return them at the last session. You won't peek — no one has to share his or her letter with anyone else unless they choose to do so. You might suggest that people also address the envelope; if they cannot attend the final session, you will mail their letter back to them.

In the letter, write about a situation in your life, your community, this nation or the world that needs healing. Perhaps it's a rupture in a relationship with a friend or family member that you long to mend, or your struggle to discover your role in eliminating poverty, homelessness or war.

Tell them to keep this assignment in the backs of their minds during this session. If anyone feels inspired at any time, take some paper and an envelope and start writing. There will be about 10 minutes at the end for everyone to write, and the facilitator/instructor can hang around until everyone is satisfied with his or her letter.

Keep these in a safe place and bring them to the final session. At the end, hand them back. Invite people to reread their letters and share, if they choose to, their situations and the insights that they gained in this class. Or, people may choose to write a private response back to themselves.

Dictionary of Peace Symbols

Calumet (peace pipe) - Calumet means "reed" in French. Such pipes were considered sacred, offering communion with the animate powers of the universe and embodying the honor and the source of power of Native Americans who possessed them. Calumets were used at the conclusion of peace treaties and in ceremonies of adoption. The pipes were principally used by the Dakotan and Algonquian peoples of the Great Plains and in the southeastern United States.

Dove - In the Bible, a dove was released from the Ark by Noah and returned with an olive branch to show that the Biblical flood was over. Ever since, the dove has symbolized deliverance and God's forgiveness.

Rainbow - The rainbow is also a biblical peace symbol. When men went off to fight they would take their "bow" with them — when they would return home they would "hang their bow" up on the wall indicate that they were not at war but in a time of peace. The rainbow is the same action by the Holy One "hanging bow" in the sky for all to see that we are in a time and promise of peace. In Christian tradition it symbolizes God's forgiveness, as it was placed in the sky as the arch of peace after the Biblical flood — a symbol of the covenant between God and humankind.

Mistletoe - "After the sun god Balder was killed by the wicked Loki's mistletoe dart, the plant was feared and hated by all as the wicked instrument of death and betrayal. But Balder's mother, the goddess Freya, redeemed it in honor of her son, decreeing that mistletoe should become a symbol of peace and reconciliation. From that time on, enemies who met under a clump of mistletoe would lay down their arms and declare a truce. That is why it is hung in the doorway to this very day, and a kiss of peace and loving kindness bestowed on all who enter." (Scandinavian folklore, cited by Susan Wittig Albert in *Mistletoe Man*.)

Olive Branch - The olive branch has for thousands of years been used as a sign of peace and goodwill. In early cultivation of the olive it took decades to bear fruit for harvest, and anyone who planted olive groves must be expecting a long and peaceful life. The symbolism is also probably related to the Biblical story of the dove. An olive branch is clutched in the right talons of the American Eagle in the Great Seal of the United States (right), symbolizing peace.

Olive Wreath - The olive wreath, like the one at left taken from the United Nations logo, was the highest award given to a citizen in ancient Greece. The prize was also given to winners at the ancient Olympic Games - a time when wars were suspended between competing states.

Peace Sign - The Peace Action Symbol was designed on February 21, 1958 for use in the first Aldermaston Easter Peace Walk in England. The symbol is the composite semaphore signal for the letters 'N' and 'D' standing for Nuclear Disarmament.

Peace Sign - This sign is thought to have begun in Europe during World War II when a V for victory was painted on walls as a symbol of freedom from occupying forces. The sign was very widely used by peace movements in the 1960s and 70s as a symbol of victory for peace and truth.

Peace Banner - Symbolizing "peace through culture," this symbol, prevalent in many cultures, was designed by artist Nicholas Roerich. More can be learned at <www.wmea-world.org/Teachings/Lectures/NR_Banner.html>

Brainstorming Exercise: Everyday Nonviolence

Time: 20 minutes
Supplies: big paper or board to write on

This exercise complements the third essay in this session, "*Human Nature Isn't Inherently Violent*," by Alfie Kohn.

Brainstorming is a lateral thinking process that asks people to come up with ideas and thoughts that seem at first to be a bit bizarre. Anything goes! After the session you can change them into ideas that are useful and original. During brainstorming sessions there should therefore be no criticism: you are trying to break down assumptions. Judgments and analysis at this stage will stunt idea generation. Ideas should only be evaluated at the end of the brainstorming session.

I introduce this session with a couple of examples of everyday nonviolent behavior that we take for granted, explaining that we read about violence in the newspaper and see it on the television news because it *is* news – something outside the norm. Our daily routine of nonviolence is *not* news – it is so common that it is boring.

There was a newspaper article about a man who was angry because his wife cooked him macaroni and cheese every night. He wanted healthier meals, so he beat her to death with a hammer. Macaroni and cheese will be served in thousands of households tonight. Most husbands who don't like it will ask for a salad, or cook dinner themselves. Asking for a salad is our natural way of nonviolence. (Write: "We ask for a salad.")

A young mother was fed up with her year-old daughter's crying, so she beat her to death, put her in a trash bag and buried her under the porch. Thousands of babies will cry tonight. Their mothers hug them and dry their tears. Hugging the baby is the natural way of nonviolence. (Write: "We hug babies.")

Use these examples — or ones from your own experience — to start a brainstorming session about everyday nonviolence. Some of the answers you might get: We vote. We go to court. We say please. We share. We take turns. We negotiate. We write letters of complaint. We get divorced. We buy things in stores. We write wills. We sign contracts. We go to counseling. We ask for help. We apologize. We count to ten and take a time out.

Keep it moving swiftly. After about five minutes wrap up the brainstorming and briefly reflect on your long list.

Group discussion: Human Nature isn't Inherently Violent

Time: 10-20 minutes
Supplies: a copy of the Seville Statement (below) for everyone

This exercise also complements the third essay in this session, "*Human Nature Isn't Inherently Violent*," by Alfie Kohn. It can be conducted in conjunction with the "Everyday Nonviolence" exercise described above, or on its own. Give everyone a copy of the statement and discuss it. If you have enough people, divide into groups and assign each group one of the statements to discuss among themselves and report back.

Seville Statement on Violence
(in plain language)

The Seville Statement on Violence is a scientific statement which says peace is possible because war is not a biological necessity. The Statement was written by an international team of specialists in 1986 for the United Nations sponsored International Year of Peace and its follow-up. The Statement was based on the latest scientific evidence and it has been endorsed by scientific and professional organizations around the world.

Introduction

This Statement is a message of hope. It says that peace is possible and that wars can be ended. It says that the suffering of war can be ended, the suffering of people who are injured and die and the suffering of children who are left without home or family. It says that instead of preparing for war we can use the money for things like teachers' books and schools and for doctors, medicines and hospitals.

We who wrote this Statement are scientists from a countries North and South, East and West. The Statement has been endorsed and published by many organizations of scientists around the world including anthropologists, ethnologists, (animal behavior) physiologists, political scientists, psychiatrists, psychologists and sociologists.

We have studied the problem of war and violence with today's scientific methods. Of course knowledge is never final and someday people will know better than we know today. But we have a responsibility to speak out on the basis of the latest information.

Some people say that violence and war cannot be ended because they are part of our natural biology. We say that is not true. People used to say that slavery and domination by race and sex were part of our biology. Some people even claimed they could prove these things scientifically. We now know they were wrong. Slavery has been ended and now the world is working to end domination by race and sex.

1. It is scientifically incorrect when people say that war cannot be ended because animals make war and because people are like animals. First it is not true because animals do not make war. Second, it is not true because we are not just like animals. Unlike animals, we have human culture that we can change. A culture that has war in one century may change and live at peace with their neighbors in another century.

2. It is scientifically incorrect when people say that war cannot be ended because it is part of human nature. Arguments about human nature cannot prove anything because our human culture gives us the ability to shape and change our nature from one generation to another. It is true that the genes that are transmitted in egg and sperm from parents to children influence the way we act. But it is also true that we are influenced by the culture in which we grow up and that we can take responsibility for our own actions.

3. It is scientifically incorrect when people say that violence cannot be ended because people and animals who are violent are able to live better and have more children than others. Actually, the evidence shows that people and animals do best when they learn how to work well with each other.

4. It is scientifically incorrect when people say that we have to be violent because of our brain. The brain is part of our body like our legs and hands. They can all be used for cooperation just as well as they can be used for violence. Since the brain is the physical basis of our intelligence, it enables us to think of what we want to do and what we ought to do. And since the brain has a great capacity for learning, it is possible for us to invent new ways of doing things.

5. It is scientifically incorrect when people say that war is caused by 'instinct'. Most sci-entists do not use the term 'instinct' anymore because none of our behavior is so determined that it cannot be changed by learning. Of course, we have emotions and motivations like fear, anger, sex, and hunger, but we are each responsible for the way we express them. In modern war, the decisions and actions of generals and soldiers are not usually emotional. Instead, they are doing their jobs the way they have been trained. When soldiers are trained for war and when people are trained to support a war, they are taught to hate and fear an enemy. The most important question is why they are trained and prepared that way in the first place by political leaders and the mass media.

Conclusion
We conclude that we are not condemned to war and violence because of our biology. Instead, it is possible for us to end war and the suffering it causes. We cannot do it by working alone, but only by working together. However, it makes a big difference whether or not each one of us believes that we can do it. Otherwise, we may not even try. War was invented in ancient times, and in the same way we can invent peace in our time. It is up to each of us to do our part.

"An Eye for an Eye Makes the Whole World Blind"   *Mohandas Gandhi*

Class of Nonviolence
Lesson 2
Gandhi

Essays for Lesson Two

Doctrine of the Sword by Mohandas Gandhi
Gandhi in the 'Postmodern' Age by Sanford Krolick and Betty Cannon
Family Satyagraha by Eknath Easwaran
Ahimsa by Eknath Easwaran
My Faith in Nonviolence by Mohandas Gandhi
Love by Mohandas Gandhi
A Pause From Violence by Colman McCarthy

Questions for Lesson Two

What do you think Gandhi would say or do
if he showed up in the United States at this time?

Gandhi believed that "poverty was the worst form of violence."
What do you think he meant?

Why did Gandhi totally reject the notion of making anyone an "enemy"?
Who was the "enemy" in Gandhi's mind?

Do you think the U.S. government in El Salvador mirrored the treatment of India by the British
during Gandhi's time?
The book, "Salvador Witness" by Ann Carrigan, on the life and death of
Jean Donovan, will help you answer this relevant question.

Describe what Gandhi meant by ahimsa and satyagraha. Do these Gandhian doctrines jibe with
his notion that it is better to resort to violence than
cowardly retreat from nonviolently confronting unjust aggression?

Who are the authors in this session?

Eknath Easwaran: was an Indian-American professor, author, translator, and religious teacher. He was influenced by Gandhi, whom Easwaran met when he was a young man.

Gandhi display/altar

For this session we like to bring a picture of Gandhi into the room so he can be with us as we gather wisdom and inspiration from him. (The famous Margaret Bourke-White photo of Gandhi and his spinning wheel at <www.kamat.com/mmgandhi/wheel.jpg> is a good choice.) If you feel comfortable doing so, you can create a little display, or altar, in the center of the circle. Artistically lay out a yard of unbleached muslin (about $1 at a fabric store) to represent Indian homespun (called *khadi)* and place upon it a couple of pictures of Gandhi, a bowl of salt to recall the salt march, perhaps a map of India. Add a picture of an Indian flag, print out a couple of quotations — use your imagination. You can light a candle or a simple oil lamp. "*When the inner lamp burns*," Gandhi once observed, "*it illuminates the whole world.*"

You can make the candle or lamp the focus of today's opening meditation. Eknath Easwaran, who wrote two of this lesson's essays, once said that a flame from a lamp, when placed outside, will flicker and may even go out in the wind. When we bring it inside and place it in a quiet alcove the flame burns steady, bright and true. When we meditate, he continued, we try to get our mind into that calm, quiet, windless place where it does not flicker and burns straight and true.

Reflective Exercise: Gandhi Said . . .

Time: 10-15 minutes
Supplies: A Gandhi quote on a slip of paper for each person

Maureen suggested this gentle way to start the session. You can cut up a copy of the readings and give each person a sentence or a short paragraph or use the pithy quotations on the next page.

Hand everyone a quotation or have them draw one from a basket. Give everyone a minute to read over his or her quotation. Then, have each person stand up and slowly and thoughtfully read their portion out loud to the group. Do this without discussion, one after another.

When all have read, provide a minute or so of reflective silence. Then, ask if anyone would like to have anything repeated, or if they found something especially memorable, confusing, inspiring, profound or meaningful to their lives. Continue the discussion for as long as it is productive.

Gandhi Said . . .

An eye for eye only ends up making the whole world blind.

A coward is incapable of exhibiting love; it is the prerogative of the brave.

An ounce of practice is worth more than tons of preaching.

As human beings, our greatness lies not so much in being able to remake the world — that is the myth of the atomic age — as in being able to remake ourselves.

Be the change that you want to see in the world.

First they ignore you, then they laugh at you, then they fight you, then you win.

I am prepared to die, but there is no cause for which I am prepared to kill.

I claim that human mind or human society is not divided into watertight compartments called social, political and religious. All act and react upon one another.

I suppose leadership at one time meant muscles; but today it means getting along with people.

It is any day better to stand erect with a broken and bandaged head then to crawl on one's belly, in order to be able to save one's head.

An error does not become truth by reason of multiplied propagation, nor does truth become error because nobody sees it.

Nearly everything you do is of no importance, but it is important that you do it.

Nobody can hurt me without my permission.

Non-cooperation with evil is as much a duty as is cooperation with good.

Poverty is the worst form of violence.

Strength does not come from physical capacity. It comes from an indomitable will.

There is a sufficiency in the world for man's need but not for man's greed.

Those who say religion has nothing to do with politics do not know what religion is.

To believe in something, and not to live it, is dishonest.

Truth never damages a cause that is just.

You must not lose faith in humanity. Humanity is an ocean; if a few drops of the ocean are dirty, the ocean does not become dirty.

Even if you are a minority of one, the truth is the truth.

Fear has its use but cowardice has none.

A 'No' uttered from the deepest conviction is better than a 'Yes' merely uttered to please, or worse, to avoid trouble.

Honest disagreement is often a good sign of progress.

In a gentle way, you can shake the world

Reflective Exercise: Namaste

Time: about 5 minutes
Supplies: None required; music (CD and player) optional

Namaste is a Sanskrit greeting that has been given various meanings:

I greet that place where you and I are one.
I salute the Light of life in you.

One that is especially meaningful in this class is:

I recognize that within each of us is a place where peace
dwells, and when we are in that place, we are One.

namaste gesture

Namaste is said with a gesture: bring both hands together, palms touching, in front of the person — usually at the chest/heart level, and bow slightly.
There is an extensive and beautiful explanation of Namaste online at <www.flex.com/~jai/articles/namaste1.html>.

Namaste is how Gandhi would have greeted people. Explain its significance and demonstrate the gesture. It is helpful to write the definition on a chalk board or tack it to the wall on a big piece of paper. Ask everyone to mill around and greet everyone else in the class with "Namaste."

It adds to the atmosphere to have meditative music playing in the background during this exercise, although it is not required. Some suggestions: Veena Prasad's "*Raghupati Raghava*," available on "Increase the Peace," available at <www.songsofpeace.org> (this was reportedly Gandhi's favorite hymn), or "*Raga Madhu Kauns*," on "Music from the Heart: A Collection of Spiritual, Ritual and Meditative Music."

Fun Reflection: An Eye for an Eye . . . .
makes the whole world blind

Time: 2 minutes
Supplies: chocolate eyeballs

It is a Hindu custom for the birthday child to give a gift of chocolate to his or her guests. In 2006 we offered this session on Gandhi's birthday, October 2, and without thinking through the implications, handed out chocolate eyeballs because they were on sale at the discount store. One student held hers up and quipped "an eye for an eye makes the whole world blind . . " which resulted in a big laugh and a lively conversation. We'll do it again.

Reflective Exercise: Seven Deadly Social Sins

Time: about 15 minutes
Supplies: a copy of the 7 deadly social sins for everyone (or post them in large print)

7 Deadly Social Sins
politics without principle
wealth without work
commerce without morality
pleasure without conscience
education without character
science without humanity
worship without sacrifice

Gandhi said, "Nonviolence is not a garment to be put on and off at will. Its seat is in the heart, and it must be an inseparable part of our being." This exercise helps bring us to a deeper understanding of the centrality of nonviolence in our everyday lives.

It is helpful to first describe the more familiar Christian list of seven deadly sins: Wrath, Avarice, Sloth, Pride, Lust, Envy and Gluttony. (To remember them, use the mnemonic WASPLEG, taken from the first letter of each sin.) These are often described as sins (or, violations of moral laws) that separate us from god, or wholeness. (Irish playwright George Bernard Shaw had his own list of the seven deadly sins: food, clothing, firing, rent, taxes, respectability and children. "Nothing," he said, "can lift those seven millstones from Man's neck but money; and the spirit cannot soar until the millstones are lifted.")

Break into smaller groups if the class is a large one. Some questions you might ask about Gandhi's seven: what makes them different from the traditional Christian sins? (one possible answer is that they are transgressions against the community.) Can you think of some examples of social sins that fall into each category? On the next page is a laid-out copy of the 7 deadlies. We print these on cardstock, cut them into strips, punch a hole in the top and tie on a short ribbon. These bookmarks are a gift to your students.

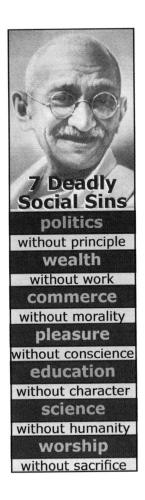

7 Deadly Social Sins

politics
without principle
wealth
without work
commerce
without morality
pleasure
without conscience
education
without character
science
without humanity
worship
without sacrifice

7 Deadly Social Sins

politics
without principle
wealth
without work
commerce
without morality
pleasure
without conscience
education
without character
science
without humanity
worship
without sacrifice

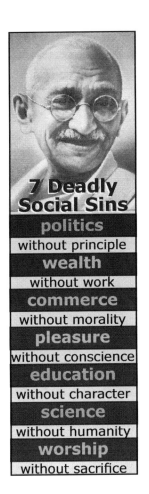

7 Deadly Social Sins

politics
without principle
wealth
without work
commerce
without morality
pleasure
without conscience
education
without character
science
without humanity
worship
without sacrifice

7 Deadly Social Sins — politics — without principle — wealth — without work — commerce — without morality — pleasure — without conscience — education — without character — science — without humanity — worship — without sacrifice

7 Deadly Social Sins — politics — without principle — wealth — without work — commerce — without morality — pleasure — without conscience — education — without character — science — without humanity — worship — without sacrifice

You can print this page on cardstock and cut it into individual bookmarks. For extra zing, punch a hole in the top and thread through a piece of colorful ribbon or yarn. It would be considered "bringing in the circus elephants" to laminate them but we have been tempted.

The peaceCENTER often puts pithy yet important information like this in a handmade bookmark format — we've run into people who have carried theirs for years.

Films for this session

Reading about Ahimsa and Satyagraha can be theoretical and abstract.
SEEING the Satyagrahi's heads bashed in brings forth gasps of shock and outrage. SEEING the Tibetan monks shed tears over endangered worms makes people laugh, then pause and think about the limits of their own compassion.

To illustrate **Ahimsa**:
Seven Years in Tibet (1997) – On the DVD, show scene 15, from the first meeting with the young Dalai Lama through the end of the second worm sequence (about 5 minutes). The Tibetan monks are unwilling to continue digging the foundation for a movie theater because worms may be hurt. The Dalai Lama explains to the European engineer (Brad Pitt) the concept of "doing no harm to any sentient being" and they find a way to work around it. We use this film clip to introduce the *Circle of Caring* exercise (page 36.)

To illustrate **Satyagraha**:
Gandhi (1982) – On the VHS tape, show 10:30 - 25:20 of tape 2 (about 15 minutes), starting with the word "SALT" and ending with the reporter phoning in his story about the Dharasana Salt Works action. On the DVD, this comprises scenes 18 (Salt March) & 19 (Dharasana Salt Works.)

We have found that the Indian's opposition to the salt tax requires explanation. After all, what's wrong with a tax? We pay taxes. These points help put it in context:

> Britain was a colonial power that exploited the Indian land and people for their own selfish benefit. The Indians had no vote about the taxes imposed on them. One of the rallying cries of our American Revolution was "no taxation without representation," which is the same situation that the Indians faced.

> Salt was plentiful and cheap in India, especially compared to the cost of extracting salt from the mines in Cheshire, England. The purpose of the tax was to make Indian salt artificially more expensive than English salt so that the English salt mine owners could continue to make profits.

*A Force More Powerful (2000): If you have time, show episode 2, about Gandhi's role in Indian independence, about 25 minutes. (The DVD can be purchased from <www.aforcemorepowerful.org>, or it may be available through your public library.)

Exercise: Circle of Caring

Time: 15-20 minutes
Supplies: Paper, crayons

In his book "Lost Boys," author James Garbarino describes a "circle of caring." For most of us, some living things lie within our circle of caring, some fall outside the circle. Some people have very small circles, some have very big ones. We call people whose circles include only themselves "sociopaths."

Garbarino describes a scene from the movie "Seven Years in Tibet" where a group of Buddhist monks take great care while digging the foundation for a new building not to kill any worms. Worms were inside their circle of caring. Where would a worm be in yours?

If the group is large enough it is more engaging to form groups of two or three and work this exercise as a team, discussing each choice among themselves. If you work in groups, provide each person with a crayon so they each have their own colors. Start with each group or person drawing a big circle on a blank sheet of paper. Ask each person to write inside the circle those beings that are inside their circle of caring. Ask them to write outside the circle those that are outside the circle. They might want to place the beings that they care about most closest to the center of the circle and beings they are ambivalent about closer to the outer edge. To start the conversation, start by quickly naming some animals: Worms. Mosquitoes. Wasps, Horses. Cows. Pigs. Deer. Cats. Dogs. Spiders. Snakes. Hamsters. Rats. Pigeons. Dolphins. A thousand year old redwood tree, the endangered northern spotted owl. Encourage them to talk about their choices among themselves. There are no right or wrong answers – this is about what YOU think.

As you go along, ask clarifying questions. Can you have compassion for an animal if you eat it? What makes us place some animals on par with family members while others fall completely outside the circle? Can there be degrees of Ahimsa (I eat chickens, but only free-range, organic ones) or is it all-or-nothing?

Now, ask each person to place these inside or outside their own circles: your family, your neighbors, the people in this room, people who live in Sweden, a drug addict, the President, an inmate on death row, a child who lives in Iraq, Osama Bin Laden, an undocumented immigrant.

Ahimsa is usually defined as the avoidance of doing harm to any sentient (having sensation of feeling) being. Is compassion the same thing as Ahimsa? Is it enough for you to avoid *doing* harm – being an active participant in harm — or could ahimsa include preventing or alleviating the harm that is done by others, by circumstances or by systems? (for example, hunger, poverty, lack of clean water or health care.)

What do our **actions** tell us about our compassion? The environmentalist Edward Abbey said, "*Sentiment without action is the ruin of the soul.*" Or Gandhi: "*Action expresses priorities.*" What do you think they meant?

In the Christian tradition it is not considered enough just to do good deeds – they must be done with love, as described in 1Corinthians 13:3: "*And though I bestow all my goods to feed the poor. . . and have not love, I gain nothing.*" Is love required for ahimsa?

Facilitator's Manual for the Class of Nonviolence

Theater: Call My Bluff Game

Time: About 10 minutes, not including the films

Supplies: None

This is a fun way to introduce the definitions of Ahimsa, Satyagraha and Mahatma. You need three "ringers" and an emcee, so it works best with a large group.

Assign each "ringer" a number, 1, 2 or 3 (that will be the number of the definition they will present) and give them enough time to absorb the definitions and make them their own. Sit them together in the circle or at the front of the class.

The emcee explains the game: each of the three "experts" will give a convincing definition of a term from the readings, but only one of the "experts" will be telling the truth — the other two are faking it. Your job is to listen to the definitions closely and at the end we will vote — by cheering, booing, stamping our feet, shouting out "true" or "false" — on which definition is correct.

After each of the actors has presented his or her definition, the emcee will call for the vote. We step behind each person; hover our palm over his or her head, summarize the definition and call for the vote ("does satyagraha mean half-naked? Let hear it!")

We start with defining Ahimsa, show the *worm* excerpt from "Seven Years in Tibet," then discuss it. After this discussion, we conduct the "Circle of Caring" exercise. Next, we define Satyagraha, show the Salt March/Salt Works clip from "Gandhi," then discuss it. Finally, we define Mahatma. After this, if there is time, you can show the Gandhi clip from "A Force More Powerful," but in a two-hour session it is unlikely that there will be time.

Our whacky definitions are on the next page; the correct definitions are in bold. As always, feel free to adapt them or to create your own.

Ahimsa *(pronounced ah-HIM-sah)*

(1) This was a popular term during Gandhi's time in South Africa and it describes people who are not native to South Africa, especially people like Gandhi, who came from India. It comes from the Latin and literally means "He is not from South Africa." It is considered a derogatory term. If we deconstruct the Latin root, "A" means "not," just like a-moral means not moral. Him means just what it sounds like – "him." The feminine version is "*aherssa.*" SA is short for South Africa.

(2) Ahimsa is an Indian song – we get our word "hymn" from the Sanskrit work ahimsa. Singing was very important in the Indian struggle for independence. When people marched in protest marches or attended rallies they sang liberation ahimsas. This was a tradition carried on by Martin Luther King when he translated nonviolence for the American struggle; hence, such great civil rights songs as "We Shall Overcome" and "Ain't gonna let nobody turn me 'round."

(3) **Ahimsa is Sanskrit for avoidance of *himsa*, or violence. It is most often interpreted as meaning peace and reverence toward all living things. Ahimsa is an important doctrine of Hinduism, Jainism, and Buddhism. Its first mention in Indian philosophy is found in the Hindu scriptures called the Upanishads, the oldest of which date to about 800 BCE**

Satyagraha *(pronounced sat-YAH-grah-hah)*

(1) **Satyagraha is the philosophy of nonviolent resistance most famously employed by Mohandas Gandhi in forcing an end to the British Raj in India and also during his struggles in South Africa. Satya means "truth" and graha means "force," so satyagraha literally means "truth-force," or the power of confronting oppressors with the truth to eliminate injustice.**

(2) A satyagraha is the white loincloth that Gandhi wore in his later years. Satya means "half" in Sanskrit and "graha" means naked, so the term literally means half-naked. This simple method of dress irritated British Prime Minister Winston Churchill, who spoke fluent Sanskrit; in 1931 he caused an international incident by calling Gandhi "a half-naked fakir."

(3) Satyagraha in India means the same thing as apartheid in South Africa: segregation of the races. Gandhi campaigned against satyagraha, which was implemented by the British rulers, known as the Raj. Satyagraha came to an end with Indian independence.

Mahatma *(pronounced mah-Hot-mah)*

(1) Mahatma was the name that Gandhi affectionately called his mother-in law. His wife Kasturba was from the prominent Hatma family and the prefix MA is an honorary term meaning Mother. It means "Mother Hatma." Confused Western journalists started calling Gandhi "Mahatma" and it stuck. His real name was Mohandas.

(2) **Mahatma is Sanskrit for "Great Soul." The closest Western equivalent is probably "saint."**

(3) Mahatma is a variety of rice grown in the Punjab area of India. It is long grain white rice that is especially good with curry.

Exercise: What is truth?

Time: About 20 minutes

Supplies: A copy of *The Blind Men and the Elephant* **or** The *Emperor's New Clothes* **or** *A Fable by Mark Twain* **and** a "truth slip" for each person (following 7 pages)

If we were to distill the wisdom of this session into one word, that word would be TRUTH. In Sanskrit, *Satya* (as in *Satyagraha*) has a deeper meaning than English typically assigns to "truth": factual, not a lie. *Satya* means "unchangeable", that which has no distortion, that which is beyond distinctions of time, space, and person, that which pervades the universe in all its constancy. It is not surprising to learn that it's root word, "*sat*," means "almighty god."

This exercise is designed to have the class think more broadly and deeply about what we mean by truth so as to better understand satyagraha.

The handouts for this exercise are on the following seven pages. The first handout consists of 20 quotations about truth. These should be cut up into individual slips and each person should have one (if you have more than 20 people it's OK for two people to have the same quote.) Three classic stories are on the next six pages. You just need one copy of these. There are two ways to conduct the exercise.

One way: Before you start the reading, ask each person to read their quotation to his or her self and silently reflect on what it means for a minute. They are going to listen to a story, and think about the story in relation to their own quotations. After the story, let them know that there will be time to discuss the meaning of the story. Read one of the stories — pick your favorite — to the entire group (this should take about 10 minutes.) Pass it around so that a few people get to read. Ask people to reflect on the story in light of their assigned quotation.

The other way: If your group is large, it can be more engaging to divide into three groups and give each group a different story to read. Give each person a quotation, as described above (it can be interesting when people in all three groups have the same quote, as both the story and the quote might take on a different meaning.) Give them 15-20 minutes (keep your eye out for the point when the conversation just begins to flag) to read the story aloud and discuss it amongst themselves. Then, have them report back to the group what they learned.

If you have a VERY ambitious group, all three of these stories could quite easily be adapted into little plays.

TRUTH SLIPS

"In a time of universal deceit, telling the truth becomes a revolutionary act."
George Orwell

"The great enemy of the truth is very often not the lie — deliberate, contrived and dishonest — but the myth — persistent, persuasive and unrealistic."
John F. Kennedy

"As long as people believe in absurdities, they will continue to commit atrocities."
Voltaire

"The world is too dangerous for anything but truth and too small for anything but love."
William Sloane Coffin

"Speak truth to Power."
Society of Friends (Quakers)

"It is error alone which needs the support of government. Truth can stand by itself."
Thomas Jefferson

"Most truths are so naked that people feel sorry for them and cover them up, at least a little bit."
Edward R. Murrow

"Believe those who are seeking the truth; doubt those who find it."
Andre Gide

"Such is the irresistible nature of truth that all it asks, and all it wants, is the liberty of appearing."
Thomas Paine

"Truth has not special time of its own. Its hour is now—always and indeed then most truly when it seems unsuitable to actual circumstances."
Albert Schweitzer

"It is one thing to show a man that he is in error, and another to put him in possession of the truth."
John Locke

"The most dangerous untruths are truths slightly distorted."
G. C. Lichtenberg

"The truth is violated by falsehood but outraged by silence."
Old adage

"All truth passes through three stages. First, it is ridiculed. Second, it is violently opposed. Third, it is accepted as being self-evident."
Arthur Schopenhauer

"Justice is truth in action."
Disraeli

"If you seek Truth, you will not seek to gain a victory by every possible means; and when you have found Truth, you need not fear being defeated."
Epictetus

"The first casualty when war comes is truth."
Senator Hiram Johnson, 1917

"The opposite of a correct statement is a false statement. The opposite of a profound truth may well be another profound truth."
Niels Bohr

"It takes two to speak the truth — one to speak and another to hear."
Henry David Thoreau

"Say not, 'I have found the truth,' but rather, 'I have found a truth.'"
Kahlil Gibran

The Blind Men and the Elephant

Long ago six old men lived in a village in India. Each was born blind. The other villagers loved the old men and kept them away from harm.

Since the blind men could not see the world for themselves, they had to imagine many of its wonders. They listened carefully to the stories told by travelers to learn what they could about life outside the village.

The men were curious about many of the stories they heard, but they were most curious about elephants. They were told that elephants could trample forests, carry huge burdens, and frighten young and old with their loud trumpet calls. But they also knew that the Rajah's daughter rode an elephant when she traveled in her father's kingdom. Would the Rajah let his daughter get near such a dangerous creature?

The old men argued day and night about elephants. "An elephant must be a powerful giant," claimed the first blind man. He had heard stories about elephants being used to clear forests and build roads.

"No, you must be wrong," argued the second blind man. "An elephant must be graceful and gentle if a princess is to ride on its back."

"You're wrong! I have heard that an elephant can pierce a man's heart with its terrible horn," said the third blind man.

"Please," said the fourth blind man. "You are all mistaken. An elephant is nothing more than a large sort of cow. You know how people exaggerate."

"I am sure that an elephant is something magical," said the fifth blind man. "That would explain why the Rajah's daughter can travel safely throughout the kingdom."

"I don't believe elephants exist at all," declared the sixth blind man. "I think we are the victims of a cruel joke."

Finally, the villagers grew tired of all the arguments, and they arranged for the curious men to visit the palace of the Rajah to learn the truth about elephants. A young boy from their village was selected to guide the blind men on their journey. The smallest man put his hand on the boy's shoulder. The second blind man put his hand on his friend's shoulder, and so on until all six men were ready to walk safely behind the boy who would lead them to the Rajah's magnificent palace.

When the blind men reached the palace, they were greeted by an old friend from their village who worked as a gardener on the palace grounds. Their friend led them to the courtyard. There stood an elephant. The blind men stepped forward to touch the creature that was the subject of so many arguments.

The first blind man reached out and touched the side of the huge animal. "An elephant is smooth and solid like a wall!" he declared. "It must be very powerful."

The second blind man put his hand on the elephant's limber trunk. "An elephant is like a giant snake," he announced.

The third blind man felt the elephant's pointed tusk. "I was right," he decided. "This creature is as sharp and deadly as a spear."

The fourth blind man touched one of the elephant's four legs. "What we have here," he said, "is an extremely large cow."

The fifth blind man felt the elephant's giant ear. "I believe an elephant is like a huge fan or maybe a magic carpet that can fly over mountains and treetops," he said.

The sixth blind man gave a tug on the elephant's fuzzy tail. "Why, this is nothing more than a piece of old rope. Dangerous, indeed," he scoffed.

The gardener led his friends to the shade of a tree. "Sit here and rest for the long journey home," he said. "I will bring you some water to drink."
While they waited, the six blind men talked about the elephant.

"An elephant is like a wall," said the first blind man. "Surely we can finally agree on that."
"A wall? An elephant is a giant snake!" answered the second blind man.

"It's a spear, I tell you," insisted the third blind man.

"I'm certain it's a giant cow," said the fourth blind man.

"Magic carpet. There's no doubt," said the fifth blind man.

"Don't you see?" pleaded the sixth blind man. "Someone used a rope to trick us."

Their argument continued and their shouts grew louder and louder.

"Wall!" "Snake!" "Spear!" "Cow!" "Carpet!" "Rope!"

STOP SHOUTING!" called a very angry voice.

It was the Rajah, awakened from his nap by the noisy argument.

"How can each of you be so certain you are right?" asked the ruler.

The six blind men considered the question. And then, knowing the Rajah to be a very wise man, they decided to say nothing at all.

"The elephant is a very large animal," said the Rajah kindly. "Each man touched only one part. Perhaps if you put the parts together, you will see the truth. Now, let me finish my nap in peace."

When their friend returned to the garden with the cool water, the six men rested quietly in the shade, thinking about the Rajah's advice.

"He is right," said the first blind man. "To learn the truth, we must put all the parts together. Let's discuss this on the journey home."

The first blind man put his hand on the shoulder of the young boy who would guide them home. The second blind man put a hand on his friend's shoulder, and so on until all six men were ready to travel together.

The Emperor's New Clothes

Long ago there lived an emperor who loved beautiful clothes so much that he spent all his money on being finely dressed. He had a different costume for every hour of the day.

One day two swindlers came to the emperor's city. They said that they were weavers, and knew how to make the world's finest cloth. This beautiful material had the magical property of being invisible to anyone who was stupid.

"It would be wonderful to have clothes made from that cloth," thought the emperor. "Then I would be able to tell clever people from stupid ones." So he immediately gave the two swindlers a great sum of money to weave their cloth for him.

They set up their looms and pretended to go to work, although there was nothing at all on the looms. They worked on the empty looms, often late into the night.

"I would really like to know how they are coming with the cloth!" thought the emperor, but he worried because anyone who was stupid would not be able to see the material. He decided to send someone else to see how the work was progressing.

"I'll send my honest old minister to the weavers," thought the emperor. "He is very sensible."
So the good old minister went into the hall where the two swindlers sat working at their empty looms. "Goodness!" thought the old minister, opening his eyes wide. "I cannot see a thing!" But he did not say so.

The two swindlers invited him to step closer, asking him if it wasn't a beautiful design. They pointed to the empty loom, and the poor old minister opened his eyes wider and wider. He still could see nothing, for nothing was there. "Gracious" he thought. "Is it possible that I am stupid? No one must know this."

"Oh, it is magnificent! The best!" said the old minister, peering through his glasses. "Yes, I'll tell the emperor that I am very satisfied with it!"

The emperor sent other officials to observe the weavers' progress. They too were startled when they saw nothing, and they too reported back to him how wonderful the material was, advising him to have it made into clothes that he could wear in a grand procession. The entire city was alive in praise of the cloth. "Magnifique! Excellent!" they said.

The swindlers stayed up the entire night before the procession was to take place, burning more than sixteen candles. They pretended to take the material from the looms. They cut in the air with large scissors. They sewed with needles but without any thread. Finally they announced, "Behold! The clothes are finished!"

The emperor came to them with his cavaliers. The two swindlers raised their arms as though they were holding something and said, "Just look at these trousers! Here is the jacket! This is the cloak!" "They are as light as spider webs!"

"Yes," said the cavaliers, but they couldn't see a thing, for nothing was there.

"Would his majesty kindly remove his clothes." asked the swindlers. "Then we will fit you with the new ones, here in front of the large mirror."

The emperor took off all his clothes, and the swindlers pretended to dress him, piece by piece. Then the emperor turned and looked into the mirror.

"Goodness, they suit you well! What a wonderful fit!" they all said. "What a pattern! What colors! Such luxurious clothes!"

"Don't they fit well?" asked the emperor.

The chamberlains who were to carry the train held their hands just above the floor as if they were picking up the cloth. As they walked they pretended to hold the train high, for they could not let anyone notice that they could see nothing.

The emperor walked in the procession, and all the people in the street said, "The emperor's new clothes are wonderful! What a beautiful jacket. What a perfect fit!" No one wanted to admit that he could see nothing, for then it would be said that he was stupid.

"But he doesn't have anything on!" said a child.

"Good Lord, let us hear the voice of an innocent child!" said the father, and whispered to another what the child had said.

"A child said that he doesn't have anything on!"

Finally everyone was saying, "He doesn't have anything on!"

The emperor shuddered, for he knew that they were right, but he thought, "The procession must go on!" He carried himself even more proudly, and the chamberlains walked along behind carrying the train that wasn't there.

by Hans Christian Andersen

A FABLE
by Mark Twain

Once upon a time an artist who had painted a small and very beautiful picture placed it so that he could see it in the mirror.

He said, "This doubles the distance and softens it, and it is twice as lovely as it was before." The animals out in the woods heard of this through the housecat, who was greatly admired by them because he was so learned, and so refined and civilized, and so polite and high-bred, and could tell them so much which they didn't know before, and were not certain about afterward. They were much excited about this new piece of gossip, and they asked questions, so as to get at a full understanding of it. They asked what a picture was, and the cat explained.

"It is a flat thing," he said; "wonderfully flat, marvelously flat, enchantingly flat and elegant. And, oh, so beautiful!" That excited them almost to a frenzy, and they said they would give the world to see it.

Then the bear asked: "What is it that makes it so beautiful?"

"It is the looks of it," said the cat.

This filled them with admiration and un-certainty, and they were more excited than ever.

Then the cow asked: "What is a mirror?"

"It is a hole in the wall," said the cat. "You look in it, and there you see the picture, and it is so dainty and charming and ethereal and inspiring in its unimaginable beauty that your head turns round and round, and you almost swoon with ecstasy."

The ass had not said anything as yet; he now began to throw doubts.

He said there had never been anything as beautiful as this before, and probably wasn't now. He said that when it took a whole bas-ketful of sesquipedalian adjectives to whoop up a thing of beauty, it was time for suspi-cion.

It was easy to see that these doubts were having an effect upon the animals, so the cat went off offended. The subject was dropped for a couple of days, but in the meantime curiosity was taking a fresh start, aid there was a revival of interest perceptible. Then the animals assailed the ass for spoiling what could possibly have been a pleasure to them, on a mere suspicion that the picture was not beautiful, without any evidence that such was the case. The ass was not, troubled; he was calm, and said there was one way to find out who was in the right, himself or the cat: he would go and look in that hole, and come back and tell what he found there. The animals felt relieved and grateful, and asked him to go at once—which he did.

But he did not know where he ought to stand; and so, through error, he stood be-tween the picture and the mirror. The result was that the picture had no chance, and didn't show up. He returned home and said: "The cat lied. There was nothing in that hole but an ass. There wasn't a sign of a flat thing visible. It was a handsome ass, and friendly, but just an ass, and nothing more."
The elephant asked: "Did you see it good and clear? Were you close to it?" "I saw it good and clear, O Hathi, King of Beasts. I was so close that I touched noses with it." "

This is very strange," said the elephant; "the cat was always truthful before—as far as we could make out. Let another witness try. Go, Baloo, look in the hole, and come and report."

So the bear went. When he came back, he said: "Both the cat and the ass have lied; there was nothing in the hole but a bear."

Great was the surprise and puzzlement of the animals. Each was now anxious to make the test himself and get at the straight truth. The elephant sent them one at a time.

First, the cow. She found nothing in the hole but a cow.

The tiger found nothing in it but a tiger.

The lion found nothing in it but a lion.

The leopard found nothing in it but a leopard.

The camel found a camel, and nothing more.

Then Hathi was wroth, and said he would have the truth, if he had to go and fetch it himself. When he returned, he abused his whole subjectry for liars, and was in an unappeasable fury with the moral and mental blindness of the cat. He said that anybody but a near-sighted fool could see that there was nothing in the hole but an elephant.

MORAL, BY THE CAT
You can find in a text whatever you bring, if you will stand between it and the mirror of your imagination. You may not see your ears, but they will be there.

Exercise: Gandhi's Nine Steps of Conflict Resolution
Time: 20 minutes (or more)
Supplies: a copy of this worksheet for each individual or group, or post large on a board

In his book **I'd Rather Teach Peace** Colman McCarthy lists nine steps based on Gandhi's teachings that can resolve conflict without violence. This steps work for problems of any scale: a squabble between pre-schoolers or a war between nations. Divide the class into small groups of 2-4 people. Discuss the steps, and come up with a few real-world examples where they can or have worked, drawing from both our daily lives and world events. Spend about 10 minutes analyzing the steps and anopther ten minutes dicsussing the results in the whole group.

AT HOME	IN MY LIFE	IN THE WORLD
1. **Define** the conflict.		
2. It isn't you against me .. it's you and me against the **problem** .. the problem is the problem.		
3. List the concerns that are **shared** in the relationship.		
4. Don't ask 'What **happened**?' Ask for a factual list of 'What did you do?'		
5. Practice active **Listening** skills..not passive hearing.		
6. Resolve conflict in a **neutral** place. Treaties are not made on the battlefield.		
7. Proceed with **doable** steps.		
8. Practice **forgiveness** skills, not vengeance urges. Forgiveness looks forward, vengeance looks backward.		
9. **Purify** our hearts. Get your own messy life in order before telling others how to live.		

BONUS ACTIVITY: A blogger known as "Dr. Druid" came up with a mneumonic device to remember these nine steps. Using the first letter of each word printed in **bold**, he recalls the sentence "**D**ancing **P**enguins **S**hould **H**ave **L**ong **N**ights **D**oing **F**ancy **P**olkas." Have each group create their own memory-jogging sentence and share it with the group. They'll never forget it.

Prayer: Gandhi's Peace Prayers

Time: 10 minutes
Supplies: copy of the prayers for everyone

Because the peaceCENTER is an interfaith organization we often incorporate prayer, when appropriate, into our classes. These are prayers that Gandhi wrote and often used in his daily prayer meetings at his ashram. They make a fitting ending meditation for this session.

Hindu Peace Prayer

I desire neither earthly kingdom, nor even freedom from birth and death. I desire only the deliverance from grief of all those afflicted by misery. Oh Lord, lead us from the unreal to the real; from darkness to light; from death to immortality. May there be peace in celestial regions. May there be peace on earth. May the waters be appeasing. May herbs be wholesome and may trees and plants bring peace to all. May all beneficent beings bring peace to us. May thy wisdom spread peace all through the world. May all things be a source of peace to all and to me. Om Shanti, Shanti, Shanti (Peace, Peace, Peace).

Islamic Peace Prayer

We think of Thee, worship Thee, bow to Thee as the Creator of this Universe; we seek refuge in Thee, the Truth, our only support. Thou art the Ruler, the barge in this ocean of endless births and deaths. In the name of Allah, the beneficent, the merciful. Praise be to the Lord of the Universe who has created us and made us into tribes and nations. Give us wisdom that we may know each other and not despise all things. We shall abide by thy Peace. And, we shall remember the servants of God are those who walk on this earth in humility and, when we address them, we shall say Peace Unto Us All.

Christian Peace Prayer

Blessed are the PEACEMAKERS, for they shall be known as The Children of God. But I say to you: love your enemy, do good to those who hate you, bless those who curse you, pray for those who abuse you. To those who strike you on the cheek, offer the other also; and from those who take away your cloak, do not withhold your coat as well. Give to everyone who begs from you; and, to those who take away your goods, do not ask them again. And as you wish that others would do unto you, do so unto them as well.

Jewish Peace Prayer

Come let us go up to the mountain of the Lord, that we may walk the paths of the Most High. And we shall beat our swords into ploughshares and our spears into pruning hooks. Nation shall not lift up sword against nation - neither shall they learn war any more. And none shall be afraid, for the mouth of the Lord of Hosts has spoken.

Shinto Peace Prayer

Although the people living across the ocean surrounding us are all our brothers and sisters why, Oh Lord, is there trouble in this world? Why do winds and waves rise in the ocean surrounding us? I earnestly wish the wind will soon blow away all the clouds hanging over the tops of the mountains.

Bahá'í Peace Prayer

Be generous in prosperity and thankful in adversity. Be fair in thy judgment and guarded in thy speech. Be a lamp unto those who walk in darkness and a home to the stranger. Be eyes to the blind and a guiding light unto the feet of the erring. Be a breath of life to the body of human-kind, a dew to the soil of the human heart and a fruit upon the tree of humility.

I offer you peace.
I offer you love.
I offer you friendship.
I see your beauty.
I hear your need.
I feel your feelings.
My wisdom flows from the Highest Source.
I salute that Source in you.
Let us work together for unity and love.
Mahatma Gandhi

Fun reflection: Optical Illusions

Time: 5 minutes
Supplies: a copy of the optical Illusions on the following page

Optical illusions are a fun way to introduce the concepts of truth and perception. Hand out the illusions as people arrive to get them thinking about the nature of truth and use them as a common frame of reference as you discuss satyagraha.

OPTICAL ILLUSIONS

An illusion is a distortion of a sensory perception. Each of the human senses can be deceived by illusions, but visual illusions are the most well known. Different people may experience an illusion differently, or not at all.
Many illusions work because
we see what we expect to see.
Others work because they are ambiguous:
there are many truths.

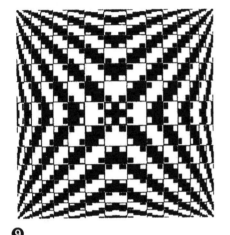

One woman - or two?

1. Are the lines parallel?
2. Do you see a young or an old woman?
3. Do you see a musician or a women's face
4. Do you see a face, or a word?
5. Do the triangle side bow in?
6. How many prongs?
7. Faces or a vase?
8. Duck or bunny?
9. Does the image bulge?

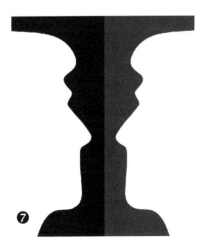

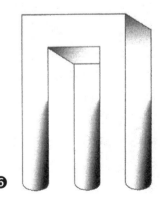

"We plant seeds that will flower as results in our lives, so best to remove the weeds of anger, avarice, envy and doubt, that peace and abundance may manifest for all."
Dorothy Day

Class of Nonviolence
Lesson 3
Dorothy Day

Essays for Lesson Three

Love is the Measure by Dorothy Day
Poverty and Precarity by Dorothy Day
Undeclared War to Declared War by Dorothy Day
This Money is Not Ours by Dorothy Day
The Scandal of the Works of Mercy by Dorothy Day
Dorothy Day by Colman McCarthy

Questions for Lesson Three

Dorothy Day, like Mother Teresa, seems to be devoted to healing the symptoms (the victim) of a sick and/or evil society rather than confronting the causes of its illness. Is this a fair assessment; and if so, what would be more fruitful to bring about change?

Dorothy Day once said of her church (Catholic Church), that, "She's a whore, but she's my mother."
Should we try to reform a corrupt institution by staying within it or is it smarter to abandon it and build a benign alternative?
Did Gorbachev's example of reforming the Soviet Union from within argue for this approach of staying "within?"

"Where there is no love, put love and you will find love" was Dorothy Day's lifelong theme.
Does it play when dealing with unresponsive individuals, the scornful homeless, violent prisoners, those who hate and revile us?

What do you think the notion of "turning the other cheek" means within the context of resisting violence and/or aggression?

Would you vote for a pacifist like Dorothy Day to rule America?
If so, why; if not, why not?

"For I was hungry, and you gave me something to eat; I was thirsty, and you gave me something to drink; I was a stranger, and you invited me in." Matthew 25:35

As with our session on Gandhi, we like to invite Dorothy Day into the room with us by bringing a picture. There are several beautiful iconic renditions:

<www.cacradicalgrace.org/conferences/politics/pics/cloud_of_witnesses/med/06%20-%20Lentz%20-%20Dorothy%20Day%20RGB.jpg>

and

<puffin.creighton.edu/jesuit/andre/images/Dorothy_Day.jpg>

and

<www.incommunion.org/forest-flier/img/dd-icon.jpg>

As we suggested in the Gandhi session, you can create a display, or altar, in the center of the circle. Include several pictures and perhaps a loaf of bread to signify hospitality, a Christian Bible opened to the Magnificat (Luke 1:46-55) to recall her faith and a newspaper to stand in for the Catholic Worker. You can also ask the students to bring with them a nonperishable food donation to be delivered to a local food bank, homeless shelter or Catholic Worker House. You can keep your Gandhi items as part of the display — just add to it at each session to reflect that each peacemaker learned from those who have gone before.

Because her Christian faith is so central to Dorothy Day's philosophy of nonviolence, we are sensitive that not everyone in the class will be Christian. Make sure that people of other faiths are not unintentionally excluded. If they feel comfortable discussing their own faith, ask them to bring their sacred texts and share some of their teaching that reflect a commitment to peace, justice, hospitality and love.

Films for this Session

*Entertaining Angels: The Dorothy Day Story

We show about a half hour of this 1996 film, from 48 minutes in (Dorothy's baptism) through 1:19 (the exit of the Cardinal, after Dorothy threatens to move her mission to Brooklyn if he insists that she take the word "Catholic" out of their name.)

You can buy the film at Vision Video <www.visionvideo.com> if it is not available at your local library.

Many of the statements/episodes in the film can spark discussion. Here are some suggestions:

(Peter Maurin): "There is no sin in being rich. There is no sin in being poor. But there is a sin in having more than you need and not sharing it with those who have less than they need." Is there enough for everyone? Do you generally operate from a sense of *abundance* or a fear of *scarcity*?

When Dorothy uses the rent money to pay for the first issue of the newspaper, Peter tells her to trust the Lord. A staff member jokes, "What if the Lord is busy this month?" Dorothy replies, "Then we are fools," and Peter adds, "Fools for Christ." (see 1 Corinthians 1:18-30 for the New Testament basis of this exchange.) What things in the readings might appear "foolish" to a "practical" person? What things in the film?

In her talk with the cardinal, Dorothy says, "If you feed the poor you're a saint; if you ask why they are poor you are called a communist." What names are used today to dismiss or demonize people who take their beliefs seriously? (For example, "naive," "crank," "tree-hugger," "bleeding heart liberal" or "politically correct.")

Dorothy Day: Don't Call Me A Saint

2006, One Lucky Dog Productions, 57 minutes. This is a new film, not yet released on DVD as of this writing, but once it is generally available it would be worthwhile to show. This is a documentary —not a dramatic recreation — and uses actual footage and photos of Dorothy Day and Peter Maurin.

This title comes from Dorothy Day herself, who said, "*Don't call me a saint. I don't want to be dismissed that easily.*" As Rosemary Berger explained in *Sojourner's Magazine*, "She didn't want recycling food from dumpsters, sleeping on a stinky prison cell floor, and getting to mass every afternoon to be dismissed as being only for special people. She had no time for halos without hard work. She practiced the Pauline understanding that *all* people of God are called to be saints — not just those with a Vatican imprimatur."

Exercise: Entertaining Angels

Time: 5 minutes
Supplies: an "Entertaining Angels" artwork (optional)

The title of the film "Entertaining Angels" comes from Hebrews 13:2 "**_Do not forget to entertain strangers, for by doing so, some have entertained angels unaware_**." It is usually illustrated by this passage from Genesis 18, in which the Patriarch Abraham comes across three strangers outside his tent:

> 1 Now the Lord appeared to him in the plains of Mamre and he was sitting at the entrance of the tent when the day was hot.
> 2 And he lifted his eyes and saw, and behold, three men were standing beside him, and he saw and he ran toward them from the entrance of the tent, and he prostrated himself to the ground.
> 3 And he said, "My lords, if only I have found favor in your eyes, please do not pass on from beside your servant.
> 4 Please let a little water be taken and bathe your feet and recline under the tree.
> 5 And I will take a morsel of bread, and sustain your hearts; after[wards] you shall pass on, because you have passed by your servant." And they said, "So shall you do, as you have spoken."
> 6 And Abraham hastened to the tent to Sarah, and he said, "Hasten three seah of meal [and] fine flour; knead and make cakes."

This has been a popular subject for artists: these are some of our favorites. You can print couple of pictures, read the story and hold a brief discussion about hospitality and its centrality to Dorothy Day's philosophy.

Chagall: <english.ucsb.edu/faculty/erickson/courses/116a/chagall_angels.jpg>
He Qi: <www.heqiarts.com/gallery/gallery1/pages/Abraham-&-three-Angels.html>
Rembrandt: <www.abcgallery.com/R/rembrandt/gelder1.html>
Psalter of St. Louis: <faculty.cva.edu/Stout/Gothic/PsalterofStLouis.jpg>

Question: Healing symptoms vs. confronting causes

Time: 15-20 minutes
Supplies: copies of the 2 stories (next page)

The first question that Colman McCarthy asks in this session is: "*Dorothy Day, like Mother Teresa, seems to be devoted to healing the symptoms (the victim) of a sick and/or evil society rather than confronting the causes of its illness. Is this a fair assessment; and if so, what would be more fruitful to bring about change?*"

Without turning this into a theological dissertation, Catholic Social Teaching distinguishes between "Works of Mercy" and "Works of Justice." Both are mandated in Micah 6:8: "*And what does the Lord require of you, but to do justice, and to love mercy and to walk humbly with your God.'*

The works of mercy are categorized as corporal (of the body) and spiritual (of the soul) The corporal works of mercy are: To feed the hungry; To give drink to the thirsty; To clothe the naked; To shelter the homeless; To visit the sick; To ransom the captive; To bury the dead. The spiritual works of mercy are: To instruct the ignorant; To counsel the doubtful; To admonish sinners; To bear wrongs patiently; To forgive offences willingly; To comfort the afflicted; To pray for the living and the dead.

The works of justice are not so neatly enumerated but rather center around "right relationship." St. Thomas Aquinas (13th Century) identified two main categories of justice. *Legal* (or general) justice is the expectation that the community will enact laws that govern its members in ways that are beneficial to everyone. *Particular* justice directs each of us to act to the good of other individuals with whom we interact. Further, Aquinas breaks justice down into two parts — *distributive* and *commutative* justice — which are typically interpreted in modern times to mean that the benefits of society are distributed with equity and that all are empowered to have a say in how this is done.

Pope Benedict's first encyclical letter (*Deus Caritas Est,* 25 December, 2005) covers this topic in depth. In it, he criticizes Marxism which, includes, he says, "...the theory of impoverishment: in a situation of unjust power, it is claimed, anyone who engages in charitable initiatives is actually serving that unjust system, making it appear at least to some extent tolerable." <www.vatican. va/holy_father/benedict_xvi/encyclicals/documents/hf_ben-xvi_enc_20051225_deus-caritas-est_en.html> Adding this dimension to the discussion would be interesting: can acts of mercy be not only incomplete but actually harmful?

 The two stories on the following page can spark discussion about these questions. You can either read them aloud as a group or divide the group in two, giving each group one of the stories to read, reflect and report.

The Starfish
Based on a story by Loren Eisley

Once a man was walking along a beach. The sun was shining and it was a beautiful day. Off in the distance he could see a person going back and forth between the surf's edge and the beach. Back and forth this person went. As the man approached he could see that there were hundreds of starfish stranded on the sand as the result of the natural action of the tide.

The man was stuck by the apparent futility of the task. There were far too many starfish. Many of them were sure to perish. As he approached the person continued the task of picking up starfish one by one and throwing them into the surf.

As he came up to the person he said, "You must be crazy. There are thousands of miles of beach covered with starfish. You can't possibly make a difference." The person looked at the man. He then stooped down and pick up one more starfish and threw it back into the ocean. He turned back to the man and said, "It sure made a difference to that one!"

The River Babies

One summer in the village, the people in the town gathered for a picnic. As they leisurely shared food and conversation, someone noticed a baby in the river, struggling and crying. The baby was going to drown!

Someone rushed to save the baby. Then, they noticed another screaming baby in the river, and they pulled that baby out. Soon, more babies were seen drowning in the river, and the townspeople were pulling them out as fast as they could. It took great effort, and they began to organize their activities in order to save the babies as they came down the river. As everyone else was busy in the rescue efforts to save the babies, two of the townspeople started to run away along the shore of the river.

"Where are you going?" shouted one of the rescuers. "We need you here to help us save these babies!"

"We are going upstream to stop whoever is throwing them in!"

Exercise: Small World

Time: 10-15 minutes

Supplies: an apple, a plastic knife and a napkin or towel for each student (we put them in a paper bag.)

We adapted the apple exercise from the teacher's guide for the PBS film "*Affluenza*." This exercise is online in its entirety at <www.pbs.org/kcts/affluenza/treat/tguide/tguide8.html>. "If the world were a village of 100 people" was originated in 1990 by Dartmouth professor Donella Meadows and has been updated since. This exercise also works well in session eight but here we use it to illustrate what Peter Maurin said in the film "Entertaining Angels": There *is no sin in being rich. There is no sin in being poor. But there is a sin in having more than you need and not sharing it with those who have less than they need.*"

Give everyone an apple and a plastic knife. Don't tell them why yet.

Leader:

"If we could shrink the earth's population to a village of 100 people, with all existing human ratios remaining the same, the village would look like this:

There would be 57 Asians, 21 Europeans, 14 Western hemisphere people (North and South Americans) and 8 Africans
70 of the 100 would be non-white
70 would be non-Christian
50% of the world's wealth would belong to 6 people — and all 6 would be U.S. citizens
70 would be able to read; 50 would suffer from malnutrition, 80 would live in substandard housing, and only one would have a university education."

Now pull out the apple and explain that we are to imagine that the apple is the earth, supporting 6.68 BILLION of these people.

Slice the apple into quarters. Set aside three of the quarters, explaining that they represent the oceans of the world. The quarter of the apple represents the land of the Earth. Invite everyone to everyone slice their own apples, setting ¾ aside.

Slice the quarter in half. Set aside one half to represent land inhospitable to people: polar areas, deserts, swamps, very high or rocky mountains. The one-eighth of the land represents where people live but not necessarily where the food is grown. Have everyone slice their own apples.

Slice this piece into four sections and set aside three of the four sections. The three sections represent areas too cold, wet, rocky, steep or with soil too poor to produce food. The remaining portion contains cities, towns, suburbs, highways, shopping centers, schools, parks, factories, parking lots and other places where people live but do not grow food. Have everyone slice their own apples.

Carefully peel the remaining slice. The apple peel represents the soil surface on which human-kind depends. It is less than five feet deep—a fixed amount of food-producing land. This fixed land is all that is available for the increasing number of people and other living things that rely on the land for food.

Open a discussion of what you have learned. Eat the apples. Dispose of your trash responsibly.

Reading the Newspaper with your Heart

Time: about a half hour

Supplies: a newspaper

How do you read the newspaper? Most of us read it for information, for news. We read it to get facts and an idea of what is going on in our world. We read it with our head. We think about it. There is a different way to read the newspaper, though. We can read it with our head *and* our hearts. At the peaceCENTER, we call this "praying the newspaper," but in a secular setting you can call it "reading the newspaper with your heart."

Bring a newspaper and hand out the whole paper, giving each person a page or a section. If the group is large, two or three people can share or you can bring more than one paper. Allow about 5 minutes for everyone to scan his or her section of the paper. Explain that they are to reflect on what is being seen and read. Suggest that they let images and impressions float to the surface. Invite peacemakers to share their discoveries, remembering that this is a time of respectful reflection. Within the conversation, if there are specific places and lives that are in need of peace or that celebrate peace that arise from the headlines, stories, ads, cartoons or pictures, encourage peacemakers to bring them into the conversation.

Typically this is a three part process. First, hold up the paper and point to the article, photo, ad or whatever captured your heart. Summarize it quickly, reading a sentence or two if it makes things clearer. The most profound reflections may come from unlikely places – the obituary of an unknown woman who brought joy into the world, the violence of language in the sports headlines, a huge selection of guns or sex for sale in the want ads.

Second, explain briefly why this story touched you: made you weep, made you angry, gave you hope. Finally, offer a prayer or a wish for the world. It helps if the facilitator goes first to model a response that is from the heart rather than the head. If others start to debate, cut it off – explain that we are taking this time to listen and reflect with respect and compassion, and then call for the next prayer or wish.

This exercise helps the group appreciate each other's joys and concerns. It models a respectful style of conversation about difficult and controversial issues. It makes a statement that this class is not about abstract theory or dusty history but rather about approaches to issues that affect us today.

At the end, let people know that they can read the newspaper with their hearts at home every morning using their own newspaper. We've done this exercise with groups as large as 500 people and it always surprises and delights us.

Discussion Starter: Stone Soup

Time: 10 minutes
Supplies: a copy of the story

The well-known "Stone Soup" story illustrates Dorothy Day's vision of hospitality as illustrated in this selection from the second essay, "Poverty and Precarity:"

> "We gave away food and more food came in—exotic food, some of it: a haunch of venison from the Canadian Northwest, a can of oysters from Maryland, a container of honey from Illinois. Even now it comes in, a salmon from Seattle, flown across the continent; nothing is too good for the poor."

Or from the first essay, "Love is the Measure":

> "St. John of the Cross said that where there was no love, put love and you would draw love out."

Read the story and discuss it in light of what you have learned about Dorothy Day.

Discussion Starter: A Sufi Story

Time: 5 minutes
Supplies: None

Sufis still invent stories about Mullah Nasrudin Hoda, a 13th Century "holy fool." This one complements Dorothy Day's essay on "Poverty and Precarity."

NASRUDIN WAS EATING a poor man's diet of chickpeas and bread. His neighbor, who also claimed to be a wise man was living in a grand house and dining on sumptuous meals provided by the emperor himself.

His neighbor told Nasrudin, "if only you would learn to flatter the emperor and be subservient like I do, you would not have to live on chickpeas and bread."

Nasrudin replied, "and if only you would learn to live on chickpeas and bread, like I do, you would not have to flatter and live subservient to the emperor."

STONE SOUP

Once upon a time, somewhere in Eastern Europe,
there was a great famine.
People jealously hoarded whatever food they could find,
hiding it even from their friends and neighbors.
One day a peddler drove his wagon into a village, sold a few of his wares,
and began asking questions as if he planned to stay for the night.

'There's not a bite to eat in the whole province,' he was told.
'Better keep moving on.'

'Oh, I have everything I need,' he said.
'In fact, I was thinking of making some stone soup to share with all of
you.' He pulled an iron cauldron from his wagon, filled it with water, and
built a fire under it. Then, with great ceremony, he drew an ordinary-look-
ing stone from a velvet bag and dropped it into the water.

By now, hearing the rumor of food, most of the villagers had come to the
square or watched from their windows. As the peddler sniffed the 'broth'
and licked his lips in anticipation,
hunger began to overcome their skepticism.

'Ahh,' the peddler said to himself rather loudly, 'I do like a tasty stone
soup. Of course, stone soup with CABBAGE — that's hard to beat.'

Soon a villager approached hesitantly, holding a cabbage he'd retrieved
from its hiding place, and added it to the pot.

'Capital!' cried the peddler. 'You know, I once had stone soup with cabbage and a bit of salt beef as well, and it was fit for a king.'

The village butcher managed to find some salt beef . . . and so it went,
through potatoes, onions, carrots, mushrooms, and so on,
until there was indeed a delicious meal for all.
The villagers offered the peddler a great deal of money for the
magic stone, but he refused to sell and traveled on the next day.

And from that time on, long after the famine had ended,
they reminisced about the finest soup they'd ever had.

Reflective Exercise: Magnificat

Time: about 20 minutes
Supplies: A copy of the Magnificat for each person; CD player and CD of Magnificat

Dorothy Day converted to Catholicism the day after the birth of her daughter, Tamar, in 1927. The "Magnificat" (also known as the *Canticle of the Blessed Virgin Mary*) is a prayer, found in Luke 1:46-55 in the Christian New Testament, and often associated with Dorothy Day. It rejoices in motherhood and gives thanks to a merciful god who scatters the proud, casts down the mighty, lifts up the lowly and fills the hungry. Scholars have noted similarities to the Song of Hannah (1 Samuel 2:1-10) which also thanks god who ". . . breaks the bows of mighty ones . . . lifts the poor up from the dust, the needy out of misery . .)

According to Luke, after the Virgin Mary was visited by the archangel Gabriel she rushed to share the good news with her cousin, Elizabeth. She felt Elizabeth's unborn son stirring in her womb (he who was to become John the Baptist) and the Magnificat poured forth. In Latin the first line is: "*Magnificat anima mea Dominum,*" My soul magnifies the Lord.

The Magnificat has been set to music more often than any Christian liturgical text other than the Mass itself. It was banned in the Guatemalan church in the 1980s because of its revolutionary message. The most famous version is probably Bach's glorious Magnificat, composed in 1723.

You will need a tape or CD of the Magnificat for this exercise. It may be available in the local library, or a classically-trained church musician could lend you one. They vary in length: Bach's is about 30 minutes, which is too long for a two-hour session. You might play the music in the background for about 15 minutes as people are arriving, pause it at track 7 to prepare for the exercise, then turn it on again at track 10 as people are leaving. Other versions are shorter: the one on Arvo Pärt's "Te Deum" (ECM 1505) performed by the Estonian Philharmonic is only 6:38, a perfect length for this exercise.

In the longer versions, each section will be on a separate track. The ones to concentrate on in Bach's Magnificat are (7) "Fecit potentiam" (*He has shown strength with his arm; he has scattered the proud in the imagination of their hearts*) (8) "Deposuit potentes" (*He has put down the mighty from their seat and has exalted the humble and meek*) and (9) "Esurientes implevit bonis" (*He has filled the hungry with good things and the rich he has sent away empty.*)

Hand everyone a copy of the Magnificat. Read over the words, slowly and deliberately. Play the music and listen to it in silence. Read the words slowly again. After the second reading you can ask the students to underline the words in the canticle that move them, surprise them or confuse them. Share their thoughts.

Concentrate on the lines that are in bold. Does this tell you anything about Mary that you didn't know? Are these the words that the Christian churches you know of live by and try to fulfill? Can you think of some examples of where they *do* fulfill Mary's prayer? Where they fall short? What does it mean to make your faith active in the world? Is there a connection between motherhood and social justice?

Magnificat

My soul proclaims the greatness of the Lord,
my spirit rejoices in God my Savior;
he has looked with favor on his lowly servant.
From this day all generations will call me blessed;
the Almighty has done great things for me and holy is his name.
**He has mercy on those who fear him,
from generation to generation.
He has shown strength with his arm
and has scattered the proud in their conceit,
Casting down the mighty from their thrones
and lifting up the lowly.
He has filled the hungry with good things
and sent the rich away empty.**
He has come to the aid of his servant Israel,
to remember his promise of mercy,
The promise made to our ancestors,
to Abraham and his children for ever.

The Golden Rule

This lesson on Dorothy Day is a good place to talk about the Golden Rule, although this discussion also fits in well with the introduction (lesson one) or next week's session on Martin Luther King, Jr. (lesson four.)

The golden rule is so simple that even a child can grasp it. Treat others the way you would like to be treated.

The golden rule is applied to small things. A **golden rule for living** advises:

> "If you open it, close it. If you turn it on, turn it off. If you unlock it, lock it up. If you break it, admit it. If you borrow it, return it. If you value it, take care of it. If you make a mess clean it up. If you move it, put it back."

But the rule works for the big things, too. In 1963, Alabama Gov. George Wallace refused to allow two African-American students to enter the University of Alabama. Soon after, President Kennedy proposed a Civil Rights Bill to Congress. He said,

> "We are confronted primarily with a moral issue. It is as old as the scriptures and is as clear as the American Constitution. The heart of the question is whether all Americans are to be afforded equal rights and equal opportunities, whether we are going to treat our fellow Americans as we want to be treated."

To apply the golden rule as one person or as an entire nation, as a people or a planet, we need imagination, courage and compassion. In big things and in small, the golden rule can be a moral compass.

Illustration: In 1961 Normal Rockwell painted a "Golden Rule" cover for the Saturday Evening Post that calls for toleration in a multicultural society through its portrayal of unity among people of many different religions, races and cultures. You can download a copy at <houses-for-peace.pbwiki.com/f/Rockwell.jpg>.

Reflections: On the next page there are two poems/ reflections/ prayers that go deeper into the meaning of the golden rule and are appropriate for reflection in a secular setting. There is also a "folk tale" that conveys the same message as Pastor Niemöller's words (thank you, Barbie, for sending me this!). Any or all of these can be read aloud at the beginning or the end of this session.

Prayer to Practice the GOLDEN RULE

May I be an enemy to no one
and the friend of what abides eternally.
May I never quarrel with those nearest me,
and be reconciled quickly if I should.
May I never plot evil against others,
and if anyone plot evil against me,
may I escape unharmed
and without the need to hurt anyone else.
May I love, seek and attain only what is good.

May I desire happiness for all and harbor envy for none.
May I never find joy in the misfortune
of one who has wronged me.
May I never wait for the rebuke of others, but always
rebuke myself until I make reparation.
May I gain no victory that harms me or my opponent.

May I reconcile friends who are mad at each other.
May I, insofar as I can, give all necessary help
to my friends and to all who are in need.
May I never fail a friend in trouble.
May I be able to soften the pain of the grief stricken
and give them comforting words.

May I respect myself.
May I always maintain control of my emotions.
May I habituate myself to be gentle, and never
angry with others because of circumstances.
May I never discuss the wicked or what they have done,
but know good people and follow in their footsteps.
Eusebius of Caesarea, 4th Century

First they came for the Socialists, and I didn't speak up,
because I wasn't a Socialist.
Then they came for the Trade Unionists, and I didn't speak up,
because I wasn't a Trade Unionist.
Then they came for the Jews, and I didn't speak up,
because I wasn't a Jew.
Then they came for me,
and there was no one left to speak up for me.
Pastor Martin Niemöller (1892–1984)

The Mousetrap

A mouse looked through the crack in the wall
to see the farmer and his wife open a package.

What food might this contain?" The mouse wondered -
he was devastated to discover it was a mousetrap.
Retreating to the farmyard, the mouse proclaimed the warning.
There is a mousetrap in the house! There is a mousetrap in the house!"

The chicken clucked and scratched, raised her head and said,
"Mr. Mouse, I can tell this is a grave concern to you, but it is of no
consequence to me. I cannot be bothered by it."

The mouse turned to the pig and told him,
"There is a mousetrap in the house! There is a mousetrap in the house!"
The pig sympathized, but said, "I am so very sorry, Mr. Mouse, but there is nothing I can do
about it but pray. Be assured you are in my prayers."

The mouse turned to the cow and said
"There is a mousetrap in the house! There is a mousetrap in the house!"
The cow said, "Wow, Mr. Mouse. I'm sorry for you,
but it's no skin off my nose."

So, the mouse returned to the house, head down and dejected,
to face the farmer's mousetrap alone.

That very night a sound was heard throughout the house —
like the sound of a mousetrap catching its prey. The farmer's wife rushed to see what was
caught. In the darkness, she did not see it was a venomous snake whose tail the trap had
caught. The snake bit the farmer's wife. The farmer rushed her to the hospital, and she
returned home with a fever.

Everyone knows you treat a fever with fresh chicken soup,
so the farmer took his hatchet to the farmyard for the soup's main ingredient.

But his wife's sickness continued, so friends and neighbors came to sit with her around the
clock. To feed them, the farmer butchered the pig.

The farmer's wife did not get well; she died.
So many people came for her funeral; the farmer had the cow slaughtered
to provide enough meat for all of them.

The mouse looked upon it all from his crack in the wall with great sadness.

Exercise: Golden Rule Cryptogram

Time: 2 minutes
Supplies: Copy of the cryptogram for every person

This can be something that you hand out at the beginning of the session as people arrive. Some folks are good at solving these, some aren't, so don't put pressure on anyone to get it done. The cryptogram and brief instructions for completing it are laid out in copy-ready format on the next page.

> ***Answer to cryptogram***: *"Do not do unto others what angers you if done to you by others." – Isocrates. Isocrates (436-338 BCE) was a Greek, a pupil of Socrates who opened the first permanent institution of higher liberal arts education.*

Exercise: The Ethic of Reciprocity

Time: 10 minutes
Supplies: Copy of the Ethic for everyone

On the next page is a copy-ready summary of the Golden Rule in nine different faith traditions. Hold a brief discussion about the universality of this "ethic of reciprocity." This can be helpful in the Dorothy Day discussion to emphasize that although the basis of *her* ethic was Christianity, other faith traditions hold similar values. As a conversation starter you might ask which ones are negative (*don't do*) and which are positive (*do unto*.)

Exercise: Playing by the Rules

Time: 15 minutes to ½ hour
Supplies: A current newspaper (optional)

The **Golden Rule** says that we should "Do unto others as you would have others do unto you." When we aren't practicing the Golden Rule we may be following a different rule. Some have even been given names:

   Iron Rule: Do unto others before they do it to you
   Brass Rule: Do good to others so that they will do good to you
   Silver Rule: Do unto others as they do it to you
   Rule of Gold: He who has the gold makes the rules
   Stone(Age)Rule: Do unto others in any way that seems to serve your interests

Make a big copy of these rules tack them up to the wall (or, provide a copy for everyone; it's laid out on the next page.) Discuss these six rules and how they differ. Come up with an example that fits each rule.

GOLDEN RULE CRYPTOGRAM

A cryptogram puzzle hides a phrase that is written in code. Each number stands for a letter of the alphabet. Crack the code and you will reveal a variation of the Golden Rule from the 4th Century B.C.E. Use the alphabet grid to help you solve the puzzle.

A	B	C	D	E	F	G	H	I	J	K	L	M	N	O	P	Q	R	S	T	U	V	W	X	Y	Z

```
__ __    __ __ __    __ __    __ __ __ __    __ __ __ __ __    __ __ __ __
10  9     3  9 21    10  9    13  3 21  9     9 21 25  2  7 18   26 25 24 21

__ __ __ __ __ __    __ __ __ __    __ __    __ __ __ __    __ __    __ __ __
24  3 20  2  7 18     8  9 13 11 15  10  9     3  2   21  9      8  9 13

__ __    __ __ __ __ __ __    __ __ __ __ __ __ __ __ __
16  8     9 21 25  2  7 18    11 18  9  5  7 24 21  2 18
```

Golden Rule: Do unto others as you would have others do unto you
Iron Rule: Do unto others before they do it to you
Brass Rule: Do good to others so that they will do good to you
Silver Rule: Do unto others as they do it to you
Rule of Gold: He who has the gold makes the rules
Stone(Age)Rule: Do unto others in any way that seems to serve your interests

THE ETHIC OF RECIPROCITY

You shall love your neighbor as yourself.
Leviticus 19.18

You shall love the Lord your God with all your heart, and with all your soul, and with all your mind. This is the great and first commandment. And a second is like it, You shall love your neighbor as yourself. On these two commandments depend all the law and the prophets."
Matthew 22.36-40

Not one of you is a believer until he loves for his brother what he loves for himself.
Islam. Forty Hadith of an-Nawawi 13

One going to take a pointed stick to pinch a baby bird should first try it on himself to feel how it hurts.
African Traditional Religions. Yoruba Proverb (Nigeria)

Ascribe not to any soul that which thou wouldst not have ascribed to thee, and say not that which thou doest not. This is my command unto thee, do thou observe it.
Bahá'í: Bahá'u'lláh, The Hidden Words, Arabic 29

One should not behave towards others in a way which is disagreeable to oneself. This is the essence of morality. All other activities are due to selfish desire.
Hinduism. Mahabharata, Anusasana Parva 113.8

Tsekung asked, "Is there one word that can serve as a principle of conduct for life?" Confucius replied, "It is the word shu—reciprocity: Do not do to others what you do not want them to do to you."
Confucianism. Analects 15.23

Be not estranged from another for, in every heart, pervades the Lord.
Sikhism

"Nonviolence means avoiding not only external physical violence but also internal violence of spirit. You not only refuse to shoot a man, but you refuse to hate him."
Martin Luther King, Jr.

Class of Nonviolence
Lesson 4
Martin Luther King, Jr.

Essays for Lesson Four
Martin Luther King, Jr. by Charles De Benedetti
Loving Your Enemies by Martin Luther King, Jr.
Declaration of Independence from the War in Vietnam
by Martin Luther King, Jr.
Pilgrimage to Nonviolence by Martin Luther King, Jr.
King and Pacifism: The Other Dimension by Colman McCarthy

Questions for Lesson Four

Why was "forgiveness" and "inclusive peacemaking" the crucial underpinning of Martin Luther King's approach to confronting a racist society?

Define and give an example of institutional racism.
How might you be contributing to such an entity unknowingly?

Do you believe affirmative action programs are justified? If so, why?

Have you tried to become personally acquainted with and appreciative of people from ethnic and racial backgrounds different from your own?
How did it change you?

King assumed the basic oneness of humanity as a means of overcoming racism. How have you advanced this notion in your life?

"The ultimate measure of a person is not where one stands in moments of comfort and convenience, but where one stands in times of challenge and controversy."   Martin Luther King, Jr.

As with our sessions on Gandhi and Dorothy Day, we like to invite Martin Luther King, Jr. into the room with us by bringing a picture. There are plenty to choose from, but a particularly apt one is of King standing pensively in front of a photo of Gandhi, at <www.warresisters.org/images/king_gandhi.jpg>.

As we suggested for the previous sessions, you can create a display, or altar, in the center of the circle. Include several pictures of people from the civil rights movement and some quotes by Martin Luther King. If you have built displays/altars in previous sessions, by this time the class should be familiar enough with the concept for you to ask each person to bring something to the table that symbolizes their understanding of King's philosophy. You can keep your Gandhi and Day items on display to provide continuity.

Reflection: Love is central to King's philosophy and it helps set the tone of this session to slowly and deliberately read a passage or two, either at the end of your silent meditation or at the beginning of your session. On the next page are two passages that we have found useful. Richard Mekdeci set King's words to music, which can make a moving conclusion to an opening meditation. It is available on the San Antonio Season for Nonviolence CD "*Peace is Our Birthright*," available from <www.songsofpeace.org>.

Love is patient; love is kind;
love is not envious or boastful
or arrogant or rude.
It does not insist on its own way;
it is not irritable or resentful;
it does not rejoice in wrongdoing,
but rejoices in the truth.
It bears all things, believes all things,
hopes all things, endures all things.
Love never ends.

And now faith, hope, and love abide,
these three; and the greatest of these is love.

1 Corinthians 13:4–8; 13

The ultimate weakness of violence
is that it is a descending spiral,
begetting the very thing it seeks to destroy.
Instead of diminishing evil, it multiplies it.

Through violence
you may murder the liar,
but you cannot murder the lie, nor establish the truth.
Through violence
you may murder the hater,
but you do not murder hate.

In fact, violence merely increases hate.
So it goes.
Returning violence for violence
multiplies violence,
adding deeper darkness
to a night already devoid of stars.

Darkness cannot drive out darkness;
only light can do that.
Hate cannot drive out hate:
only love can do that.

MARTIN LUTHER KING, JR.,
Where Do We Go from Here: Chaos or Community? 1967

Films for this session

We have found that films about the lunch counter sit-ins are the ideal illustration of King's six principles and six steps of nonviolence, critical to understanding of the practice of nonviolence.

In San Antonio there has been a creeping militarization of our annual Martin Luther King march, the largest in the nation: fighter jet flyovers, military recruiters invited to set up booths at the march's end point and armed junior ROTC units leading the march, to cite just three examples. King's role as an anti-war leader is less known than his role as a civil rights leader, and in this class you have the opportunity to remedy that deficiency.

If you have the time, it would be well worth your while to hold two sessions on King: one on the general principles of nonviolence and the civil rights movement and a second session just on King and war.

Emphasis on the civil rights movement
*Force More Powerful (available from <www.aforcemorepowerful.org>) – Episode One, *We Were Warriors*: Nashville Sit-ins. 25 minutes. (See pages 76-77 for an exercise using this episode.)
*Eyes on the Prize: Episode Three, *Ain't Scared of Your Jails (1960-61).* This PBS film series is available in most public libraries. (The lunch counter sit-in section of this 58-minute documentary comprises about the first 20 minutes.
February One (available from <www.newsreel.org/nav/title.asp?tc=CN0170>)
A 61-minute documentary about the Greensboro, NC lunch counter sit-ins.

Emphasis on King and war:
King: Man of Peace in a Time of War (2007) - This new hour-long documentary covers the civil rights movement but also pays close attention to King's anti-war activities. Especially interesting is a complete 1967 interview on the Mike Douglas Show where he speeks informally and articulately about the war. This show plus the scene preceeding it that directly addresses his anti-war stance is about 25 minutes (scences 4-6.) You can get it at Amazon.com for less than $15.
*Citizen King: is a two-hour PBS documentary about King's life between the Lincoln Memorial speech in 1963 and his assassination in 1968. In the last third of the film there is a brief (about 10 minute) section on his opposition to the Vietnam War, his speech at Riverside Church and the (mostly negative) reaction of other civil rights leaders to his anti-war activism. If it's not available in your public library you can buy it through PBS <www.shoppbs.org>.
*Beyond Vietnam — A Time to Break Silence, delivered 4 April 1967 at a meeting of Clergy and Laity Concerned at Riverside Church in New York City. An audio MP3 file is available for download at: <www.americanrhetoric.com/speeches/mlkatimetobreaksilence.htm>. It's 54 minutes, too long for group listening. Refer students to this site to listen on their own, or play the first few minutes so they can get a feel for the cadence of King's language.
*Eyes on the Prize II, Episode Four: "*The Promised Land*" (1967-1968). The first 10 minutes of this episode show excerpts of King delivering his major Vietnam speeches (Ebenezer Baptist and Riverside Church) and describes how his courageous stance ruined his relationship with President Lyndon Johnson and many civil rights leaders. This may be available at your public library, or used copies are sometimes available at a reasonable cost.

Musical Interlude: Music of the Civil Right Movement

Time: 15 minutes
Supplies: CD player or tape deck, music

Music and group singing were important components of the civil rights movement and we like to reflect that by incorporating music into this session. We point out that most of the civil rights movement songs were rewritten hymns or labor songs so that everyone knew the tunes; we, too, have the power to rewrite popular songs.

We highlight some of the characteristics of effective movement songs: simple, easy to learn tunes; repetitive and frequent choruses; often "call and response" so that everyone can partici-pate, short verses that are easily adapted to local situations. We also emphasize that the music was often a group experience: not a concert or elaborate choral works backed by professional musicians.

*Sing for Freedom: *The story of the Civil Rights Movement Through its Songs* (1990, Smith-sonian/Folkways Records) is an excellent resource. There is a companion book of the same name edited by Guy and Candy Carawan (1990, Sing Out Publications.) These may be avail-able from your public library but both are worthy of adding to your personal collection. (You can download individual tracks from <iTunes.com> for 99¢ each.)

Everyone should have the experience of singing "*We Shall Overcome.*" Gather everyone into a circle, join hands and sing a few verses together so that NEXT time they'll know what to do.

If you have time, play a song referencing the lunch counter sit-ins (perhaps "I'm Gonna Sit at the Welcome Table") and one for the Freedom Rides (maybe "Which Side Are You On," an old labor song rewritten by James Farmer while in jail after his participation in one of the rides.)

You can also play this CD as people are gathering and as they leave. If you have an experi-enced song leader in your group, so much the better: dispense with the prerecorded music and belt it out it live!

Reflective Exercise: Love Collage

Time: ½ hour – 45 minutes
Supplies: Paper, scissors, lots of old magazines, glue sticks, crayons or markers

Love is a misunderstood concept in the peace movement, often banally reduced to "let's all hold hands and sing Kum-ba-yah" or the motto of a popular seafood chain, "peace, love and crabs." Love is seen as mushy, what King dismissed as "some sentimental or affectionate emotion." This exercise helps the group clarify what Martin Luther King meant when he spoke of love.

First, briefly review the three kinds of love that King defines in his essay "Pilgrimage to Nonviolence," excerpted from "Stride Toward Freedom": eros, philia and agape (pronounced ah-GAH-pay.) It's in the fifth point: *"nonviolent resistance avoids not only external physical violence but also internal violence of spirit."* We usually stress the reciprocity of *philia* relationships and give (or elicit) some examples—team spirit, camaraderie, the love of parents for children, and children for parents; friendship—and also indicate that one of the traditional English translations of agape is "charity," or loving-kindness.

It is more engaging if this is done in groups of two or three, as the participants can discuss among themselves what they discover as they cut-and-paste.

Give each group a piece of paper, a glue stick, scissors and a stack (at least three or four) of magazines (make things easier on yourself by asking everyone to each bring in some old magazines.) Ask them to take about 15 minutes and make a collage illustrating the three different kinds of love that King defined. Be imaginative: go three-dimensional if you want, use words, symbols, crayons.

At the end of 15 or 20 minutes, ask the groups to describe their collages. An intriguing question: what images were easiest to find? Which ones were hardest to find? Why do you think that is? If people haven't finished their collages by the end of the exercise, they can work on them as they are participating during the remainder of the session.

Time saver: If you don't want to spend this much time on this exercise, the week before you can ask each student to bring one or two photos from magazines or Web sites that illustrate each of the kinds of love, based on their understanding from the readings. Make your collage as a group (or several collages if the group is large.) This can be completed in about half the time.

Love, Power and Justice Bookmarks

On page 86 you will find a sheet of six bookmarks that contain a Martin Luther King quotation about the intersection love, power and justice. Print these out on cardstock and cut them into individual markers. If you are feeling artistic, punch a hole in the top and thread a colorful ribbon or a piece of yarn through the top. This provides a fitting segue to the next session, where we will discuss women, power and peace.

Brainstorm: The Beloved Community

Time: 15-20 minutes
Supplies: chalkboard or big paper

One of Colman McCarthy's questions for this session is: "*King assumed the basic oneness of humanity as a means of overcoming racism. How have you advanced this notion in your life?*" One of the ways we approach this question is through a discussion of "the beloved community."

In one of his first published articles Martin Luther King, Jr. stated that the purpose of the Montgomery bus boycott "is reconciliation, . . . redemption, the creation of the beloved community."

A clue to King's definition of this beloved community lay in his distinction between desegregation and integration. Desegregation, he wrote, eliminates discrimination against blacks in public accommodations, education, housing and employment. Integration, however, is "the positive acceptance of desegregation and the welcomed participation of Negroes in the total range of human activities." Desegregation can be brought about by laws. Integration required a change in personal and social relationships.

King said desegregation will only produce "a society where men are physically desegregated and spiritually segregated, where elbows are together and hearts apart."

Another clue to the difference can be gleaned from the Latin etymology of the words:
> **segregate**: separation from the flock
> **Integrate**: to make whole

A beloved community is therefore one that has been made whole. When the community is not whole the *entire* community broken and incomplete, King maintained.

What would our beloved community look like? How can we "welcome Negroes – everyone! - into the total range of human activities?" Is this something we can do as individuals? Within our voluntary associations? Through government and laws? Brainstorm ideas and write them on the board or paper.

Exercise: The Six Steps & Principles

Time: 45 minutes

Supplies: Nashville Sit-in episode form "*A Force More Powerful*" film; list of six steps of nonviolent social change and six principles of nonviolence (on the next page)

The Nashville Sit-in episode from "*A Force More Powerful*" is a perfect case study on how conduct a nonviolent resistance campaign.

It's easier for everyone to focus if you have half the group concentrate on the nonviolent steps and the other half on the nonviolent principles. Hand out the worksheet and give them a few minutes to become familiar with the lists. Explain that we are going to watch a film about the Nashville sit-ins and, as we watch, make note of how and when the Nashville students followed the steps and principles. After the film is over, reassemble the small groups for about 5 minutes to discuss and consolidate their findings, and then have them report back to the group.

SIX PRINCIPLES OF NONVIOLENCE

Fundamental tenets of Dr. King's philosophy of nonviolence described in his first book, Stride Toward Freedom. The six principles include:

.

(1) Nonviolence is not passive, but requires courage;

(2) Nonviolence seeks reconciliation, not defeat of an adversary;

(3) Nonviolent action is directed at eliminating evil, not destroying an evil-doer;

(4) A willingness to accept suffering for the cause, if necessary, but never to inflict it;

(5) A rejection of hatred, animosity or violence of the spirit, as well as refusal to commit physical violence; and

(6) Faith that justice will prevail.

SIX STEPS OF NONVIOLENT SOCIAL CHANGE

A sequential process of nonviolent conflict-resolution and social change based on Dr. King's teachings. The Six Steps of Nonviolence developed by The King Center include:

(1) Information gathering and research to get the facts straight;

(2) Education of adversaries and the public about the facts of the dispute;

(3) Personal Commitment to nonviolent attitudes and action;

(4) Negotiation with adversary in a spirit of goodwill to correct injustice;

(5) Nonviolent direct action, such as marches, boycotts, mass demonstrations, picketing, sit-ins etc., to help persuade or compel adversary to work toward dispute-resolution;

(6) Reconciliation of adversaries in a win-win outcome in establishing a sense of community.

*From: **The King Center**, www.kingcenter.org*

Can you find all 16 words that are hidden in the heart?
All of these words have something to do with nonviolence.

ACTIVIST: one who seeks change through action.

AGAPE: the purely spiritual love of one person for another. This love corresponds to the love of God for humankind.

AHIMSA: (from the Sanskrit, ' not harming'). Avoiding injury to any sentient creature through act or thought.

CIVIL DISOBEDIENCE: The refusal to obey laws that are regarded as unjust.

JUSTICE: a fair distribution of benefits and burdens.

MAHATMA: an honorary title meaning "great soul."

MEDIATION: A process in which a neutral third party assists disputing parties in reaching a mutually acceptable settlement.

NONVIOLENCE: is a kind of persistent, disciplined, assertive and often courageous good will; is active confrontation with evil that respects the personhood of an enemy; seeks both to end the oppression or threat of violence and to reconcile the adversary.

PACIFIST: someone opposed to violence, especially war, as a means of settling disputes.

PEACE: Peace is not the absence of violence or conflict but the presence of compassionate, all-inclusive love that engages the world and relationships.

PILGRIMAGE: journey to a sacred place.

PRAY: call upon a higher power.

RECONCILIATION: restoration to harmony.

RESISTANCE: the action of opposing something that you disapprove or disagree with.

SATYAGRAHA: The term that is translated variously as "soul force" or "truth force"; the term Gandhi used to describe the power of nonviolent resistance to oppressive social structures.

VIGIL: To stand watch, usually in silence.

Exercise: Heart of Nonviolence

Time: 5 minutes

Supplies: copy of the word search puzzle (previous page) for each person

Hand these out as people arrive for their amusement and edification.

Exercise: Racism

Time: 10-15 minutes

Supplies: statements about other races (next page) cut into slips

One of the questions Colman McCarthy asks for this session is: "*Define and give an example of institutional racism. How might you be contributing to such an entity unknowingly?* "Racism is not clearly defined in the readings and the discussion can be more productive if the class has command of several definitions.

We adapted this group exercise from "*Even the Stones Will Cry out for Justice*," an adult forum on institutionalized racism published by the Evangelical Lutheran Church in America (1998) (you can buy a copy of the entire study at <www.augsburgfortress.org/store/item.jsp?redirected=true&clsid=129953&isbn=6000107617>)

Write these definitions on a chalkboard or on large paper. Cut the "statements about other races," on the next page into individual slips. Divide the class into several (at least two) groups and divvy up the slips among them. Give each group 5-10 minutes (keep an eye on them to see when the conversation flags) to categorize each of the statements into one of the definitions. There might be more than one correct category. Allow time for discussion and then pose Colman's question about our complicity in institutional racism.

> *Answer key:*
> *Racism: 5,8*
> *Race Prejudice: 1,2*
> *Race Discrimination: 3,10*
> *Stereotyping:4,9*
> *Institutional Racism 6,7*

Additional Curriculum Resource: The Shadow of Hate

If your group wants to pursue this topic we recommend *The Shadow of Hate*. It's available from Teach Tolerance, <www.tolerance.org/teach/resources/shadow_of_hate.jsp>, this kit contains a 40-minute VHS tape that explores the 300-year history of intolerance in America; a teacher's guide with 15 lesson plans and a 128-page student text. It's free for certain teachers and youth leaders and $30 for others.

Racism

Race prejudice plus the power and influence of systems and institutions to support that prejudice.

Race Prejudice

Irrational and hostile behavior toward people of a particular race about which one possesses ideas, opinions and judgments without sufficient knowledge.

Race Discrimination

The act or intention of making prejudicial generalizations about another race in order to accuse or devalue a person of a different race. This provides direct influence over a person's ability to access services or make a living.

Stereotyping

To have a fixed notion or conception of a person, group or idea allowing no individuality or critical judgment of individual cases or circumstances.

Institutional Racism

Racism as it appears and is interwoven and operative within and through institutions. Institutions are established using values and norms of the dominant culture. Institutions decide who receives career opportunities, training and skills, medical care and formal education and therefore institutions have power to reward or penalize, to provide opportunities for some and to deny them to others.

1. The shopkeeper does not allow more than two African-American youth in her shop at a time.

2. The pastor did not invite his Arab-American neighbor's children to attend vacation bible school because he assumed they were Muslim.

3. The shopkeeper did not invite the young Latino boy to apply for the job because Latinos are lazy.

4. Asians are the exemplary minority because they are all smart and hard working.

5. The supervisor didn't tell Carlos about the promotion opportunity in North Dakota because she thought he would not want to move to a city where there were few Mexican-Americans.

6. When the Congressional districts were redrawn, what had been a powerful bloc of support for Latino and African-American candidates was eliminated.

7. When the African-American high school student drives to visit his friend in a predominately white neighborhood he gets pulled over by the police who want to know if he is "lost."

8. The assignment was to do a report on a hero. When asked why Nikki only got a C on her well-written report on Jim Thorpe, the Native-American Olympic runner, her teacher responded "Jim Thorpe is not a hero."

9. All African-American families struggle for survival.

10. Despite many attempts and providing the lowest bids, the African-American owned construction company could not get the job of building new schools in the community.

Deeper Discussion: Affirmative Action

Time: 15 minutes
Supplies: None

One of Colman McCarthy's questions for this session is: *"Do you believe affirmative action programs are justified? If so, why?"* This question has generated some of the most heated and divisive discussions in the entire curriculum.

Martin Luther King's own words are sometimes twisted to use against affirmative action: *"I have a dream that my four little children will one day live in a nation where they will not be judged by the color of their skin but by the content of their character."* We are certain that King's dream was a hope for a future society free of racism: a call for the end of racial discrimination, not for the end of redress in a discriminatory society.

It is useful to start with a definition: *Affirmative action is a policy or a program providing advantages for people of a minority group who are seen to have traditionally been discriminated against, with the aim of creating a more egalitarian society. This consists of preferential access to education, employment, health care, or social welfare.*

Perhaps a more meaningful question could be: *"If there were no laws such as affirmative action holding universities and employers accountable for who they admit and hire, would the commitment to not discriminate become meaningless and would organizations drift back to being mostly white and male?"*

It can also useful to start the discussion with some examples of situations where employment and college admissions are influenced by segregation or vestiges of racism. For example:

> By some estimates, as many as 4/5 of all jobs openings are never made public: they are filled through informal networks, such as friends, relatives, neighborhoods, churches, and other voluntary associations, many of which remain deeply segregated.

> Legacy preferences, given by educational institutions to applicants based on a familial relationship to alumni, account for 10% to 15% of Ivy League university admissions. One study found this to be equal to a 160-300 point boost in SAT scores. Social groups who have education get an advantage in passing it onto their children.

After the historical and sociological basis for affirmative action laws are established the discussion can be much more productive. This is a discussion where everyone needs to keep their critical thinking caps on.

Exercise: Budget Priorities Game

Time: 15-20 minutes

Supplies: 35 beans, a game board (following page) for each group and a copy of "Where your income tax goes" from the War Resistors League, at <www.warresisters.org/> for each person

"We do not have a money problem in America. We have a values and priorities problem." *Marian Wright Edelman*

"When machines and computers, profit motives and property rights, are considered more important than people, the giant triplets of racism, extreme materialism, and militarism are incapable of being conquered. A true revolution of values will soon cause us to question the fairness and justice of many of our past and present policies." *Martin Luther King, Jr.*

This is an abbreviated version of a much more elaborate simulation developed by the Lutheran Peace Fellowship. You can get the full game at <www.lutheranpeace.org>, including a free interactive computer program that can be projected on a screen as a group exercise. All of the data is from the 2006 budget, extracted from the Federal budget, <www.whitehouse.gov/omb>.

Every group of 2-5 people should have 35 dried beans and a copy of the game board reproduced on the following page. Allow time for conversation.

The Leader says: The budget of the Federal government authorizes the spending of more than three trillion dollars each year. Of that, two-fifths is in trust funds like Social Security. The remaining three-fifths is what Congress votes on each year — it's called "discretionary spending."

More than 675 billion dollars goes to protect the United States from threats from abroad. Homeland security — protection from security threats inside our borders — is covered by a different part of the Federal budget.

Protection-related spending falls into three broad categories, shown on your game boards.

(1) **Military Force**: includes maintaining the army, navy, air force and marines and paying for troops, equipment and supplies sent to other countries. It also includes the costs of threatening to use or actually using force in response to those who would attack the United States or its allies.

(2**) Nonviolent means**: includes sending ambassadors and negotiators to help resolve conflicts. It also includes training and supporting peacekeepers to help control conflicts. The purpose is to keep disputes and conflicts from becoming violent.

(3) **Prevention**: This includes activities like the Peace Corps and all forms of aid to help solve problems in other countries – medical, construction, food production, water supply, pollution control, disease prevention. The purpose is to deal with conditions that might cause people to resort to violence.

At this point every person or group should count out 25 of their beans.

Leader: You are in charge of the Federal budget and you have 675 billion dollars to spend on these three categories. It's up to you. Each bean represents 27 billion dollars. Take a few minutes and make your budget by placing your beans on the circles.

Ask for feedback about how the money was spent, and why.

Leader: Now, clear your boards. Distribute your beans again, but this time try to predict how the government actually allocated your money.

Allow a few minutes for this.
Leader: Here's how the money is actually spent:

Take 24 of your 25 beans and dump them all into the MILITARY FORCE circle. Take the one remaining bean and put it on the border between the NONVIOLENT MEANS and PREVENTION circles – they have to share their bean. If we could split the beans *(if you want to be dramatic, bring a hammer and smash a bean)* You could actually put another half of a bean into the Military Force circle and drop the remaining crumbs into the other two circles.

But this is not the entire story. We need to add beans to cover the cost of the wars in Afghanistan and Iraq that is not included in the budget. So, take four more beans and add them to the Military Force circle. Also, we need to include the interest on the federal debt that pays for past military spending. That's six more beans to put in the Military Force.

Allow some time for discussion then give everyone a copy of the handout, "Where your income tax money really goes." (If anyone asks, Homeland Security in 2006 was just under $34 billion, a bean and a bit.)

Another excellent resource is The **National Priorities Project**, <www.nationalpriorities.org> which has even more detail about where our tax money goes. This is where we learned that the average taxpayer in San Antonio pays $2,377 in Federal Income Tax, of which $645 goes to pay for the military and $216 for interest on the military debt. There is also a section on "tradeoffs." Taxpayers in Susan's Texas Congressional District 21 contributed $483.9 million toward the war in Iraq for fiscal year (FY) 2007, This money could have provided (just a few of many examples) 198,114 children with health care or 5,770 affordable housing units. If you have the time and the inclination, localized numbers from this Web site can bring the numbers home.

PROTECTION-RELATED SPENDING

MILITARY FORCE

Weapons & Personnel
Military Aid

NONVIOLENT MEANS

Diplomacy
Peacekeeping

PREVENTION

Peace Corps
Foreign Aid

1 bean = $27 Billion

Power without
love is reckless and
abusive, and love
without power is
sentimental and
anemic.
Power at its
best is love
implementing
the demands
of justice, and
justice at its best
is power correcting
everything that
stands against
love.

Martin Luther King, Jr.
Where Do We Go From Here?
(1967)

Power without
love is reckless and
abusive, and love
without power is
sentimental and
anemic.
Power at its
best is love
implementing
the demands
of justice, and
justice at its best
is power correcting
everything that
stands against
love.

Martin Luther King, Jr.
Where Do We Go From Here?
(1967)

Power without
love is reckless and
abusive, and love
without power is
sentimental and
anemic.
Power at its
best is love
implementing
the demands
of justice, and
justice at its best
is power correcting
everything that
stands against
love.

Martin Luther King, Jr.
Where Do We Go From Here?
(1967)

Power without
love is reckless and
abusive, and love
without power is
sentimental and
anemic.
Power at its
best is love
implementing
the demands
of justice, and
justice at its best
is power correcting
everything that
stands against
love.

Martin Luther King, Jr.
Where Do We Go From Here?
(1967)

Power without
love is reckless and
abusive, and love
without power is
sentimental and
anemic.
Power at its
best is love
implementing
the demands
of justice, and
justice at its best
is power correcting
everything that
stands against
love.

Martin Luther King, Jr.
Where Do We Go From Here?
(1967)

Power without
love is reckless and
abusive, and love
without power is
sentimental and
anemic.
Power at its
best is love
implementing
the demands
of justice, and
justice at its best
is power correcting
everything that
stands against
love.

Martin Luther King, Jr.
Where Do We Go From Here?
(1967)

"I myself have never been able to find out precisely what feminism is; I only know that people call me a feminist whenever I express sentiments that differentiate me from a doormat or a prostitute."
Rebecca West

Class of Nonviolence
Lesson 5
Women, Violence, Peace and Power

Essays for Lesson Five
Feminism, Peace and Power by Mary Roodkowsky
Rape is all too Thinkable for Quite the Normal Sort of Man
by Neal King and Martha McCaughey
To the Women of India by Mohandas Gandhi
Narrowing the Battlefield by Carol Ascher
Patriarchy: A State of War by Barbara Hope
An American Shero of 1941 by Colman McCarthy

Questions for Lesson Five

Given the chance, are women just as prone to violence as men?
Is it beyond men's capacity to establish a peaceful world?
Are women's views of peace different from men;
after all, don't women expect men to "protect" them at all costs?

If a woman is in a man's apartment after a date,
a night of partying at 3 a.m.,
should she be surprised if "date rape" occurs?

In what sense is sexism a justice related issue?

Men's liberation must accompany women's liberation. Explain.

Sexual stereotypes are created and sustained by society.
Why do you think this is true and why do people go along with it?

"When any relationship is characterized by difference, particularly a disparity in power, there remains a tendency to model it on the parent-child-relationship. Even protectiveness and benevolence toward the poor, toward minorities, and especially toward women have involved equating them with children." Mary Catherine Bateson

If every woman victimized by domestic violence last year were to join hands in a line, the string of people would expand from New York to Los Angeles and back again. *(Senate Judiciary Committee, July 31, 1990)*

Someone, empowered by this class, may speak out about her (or his) abuse for the first time. It can be intense, and you will want to help, but remember that you are not a therapist and this is not a therapy group. If things look like they are moving beyond your and the class's level of comfort and competence, compassionately wind down the conversation and pass on the phone number for the 24-hour

Domestic Abuse Hotline, 1-800-799-SAFE (7233)

or to a local support group.

Who are the authors for this session?

Mary Roodkowsky: is the associate director of the United Nations Development Group (UNDG)

Martha McCaughey: is the director of Women's Studies at Appalachian State University. Her research and writings have dealt extensively with evolutionary psychology as applied to gender.

Neal King: is Associate Professor of Interdisciplinary Studies at Virginia Tech. His research interests include media violence, religious elements of popular culture, social inequality, and violent crime.

Carol Ascher: is an anthropologist whose research focus has been issues of educational equity, including desegregation, school finance, and improving schools serving low-income children of color. She is a senior research scientist at the Institute for Education and Social Policy of the New York University.

Barbara Hope: is a clinical social worker at the Harrington Family Health Center, a rural center in Downeast Maine and a survivor of childhood sexual abuse.

Display/altar

There are three main threads to the readings: women as victims of violence; women as peace-makers; and the role of power, both personal and systemic, in these gender-related issues. You'll want to reflect all three threads in your display/altar. Some literature from a local domestic violence prevention program (get enough for everyone to take one home) and a list of the women who have won the Nobel Peace Prize <nobelprize.org/nobel_prizes/peace/laureates/> are a good start. There's also a more comprehensive list of "heroines of peace" on the Nobel site at <nobelprize.org/nobel_prizes/peace/articles/heroines/index.html>. Photos of women working today for peace and justice can also be potent symbols: Women in Black, Code Pink, Mothers of the Plaza, Women's International League for Peace and Freedom, National Organization for Women, Gold Star Families for Peace, League of Women's Voters, to name a few. If your group is amenable to homework, ask each person to bring the name or a photo of a women's group working for peace and justice, or the name or photo of a woman peacemaker.

Films for this session:

*Diamonds, Guns and Rice: **Sierra Leone and the Women's Peace Movement** 2006, 58 minutes. This DVD is bundled with a curriculum guide, "**Speaking Out: Women, War and the Global Economy**." At only $19.95 it's a bargain. If you do not have time to show the entire video, we recommend the last section of the film, labeled "peace" (about 14 minutes) which covers the women's peace and justice movement, the reintegration of child soldiers and the truth and reconciliation process. It's powerful stuff.

*PeacexPeace: Women on the Frontlines 2005, 82 minutes, available from <www.peacexpeace.org/involved/host.asp> PeacexPeace follows five stories of women making peace in Burundi, Afghanistan, Bosnia-Herzegovina, Argentina and the United States (September 11 Families for Peaceful Tomorrows). Because it is divided into episodes, it lends itself to showing one section (about 15 minutes) in the class. You can read a summary of each episode at <www.peacexpeace.org/resources/DocumentarySynopsis.pdf> A DVD or VHS is available for a $50 donation to the organization.

*Peace is a Women's Job
2004, 50 minutes, available from <www.peaceisawomensjob.com>. This is a docudrama about the life of Jeannette Rankin, the subject of the last essay in this section, "*An American Shero of 1941*." The entire film is well worth watching, but if time is short, start at about minute 32, when the newly-elected congresswoman is discussing her speaking tour with her brother, to the end (about 18 minutes.) This covers her courageous and controversial vote against US entry into WWI.

More video ideas:

UNESCO has a three-hour streaming video (WMV format) of a 2007 International Women's Day panel online at <portal.unesco.org/en/ev.php-URL_ID=36807&URL_DO=DO_TOPIC&URL_SEC-TION=201.html> This is much too long for a class, but scroll down to the interview with Swanee Hunt, former US Ambassador to Austria and founder of the Initiative for Inclusive Security. It's a wonderful summary of women peacemakers, and only six minutes long.

Amnesty International's "Stop Violence Against Women Campaign" has many video stories of activist women at <web.amnesty.org/actforwomen/stories-index-eng>. This is streaming media and cannot be saved for later showing.

Group Exercise: She said . . .

Time: 15-20 minutes
Supplies: Women's peace and justice quotations (next 2 pages)

As we described in the "*Gandhi Said*" exercise in lesson two, cut these quotations into individual slips, pass them out, and have each person stand and read their quotation slowly and deliberately. After everyone has read a quote, ask if there are any reflections about a phrase that moved you, angered you or confused you, humored you or one that you would like to have repeated. Is there anything in any of these quotations that speaks to you about the role of women as peacemakers? Could a man have said this just as convincingly or is it said from a uniquely female perspective?

Exercise: Nobel Women Word Search Puzzle

Time: 5 minutes
Supplies: A copy of the Word Search puzzle for each student (page 93)

Puzzles such as this — word searches, crosswords and cryptograms — engage the brain in a different way than just reading and talking. Although they are especially appealing for younger students, adults like them, too! Hand this out at the beginning of the session, as people are gathering and let them work it out on their own. Later, you can discuss the women who have won the prize: what do they have in common? How are they different? 94 prizes have been awarded to individuals since 1900: are only 12% of the world's peacemakers women?

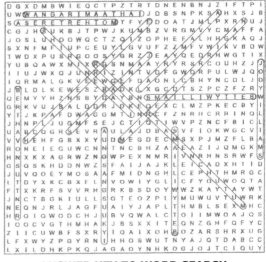

ANSWER KEY TO WORD SEARCH

Facilitator's Manual for the Class of Nonviolence

SHE SAID . . .

I have noticed that as soon as you have soldiers the story is called history. Before their arrival it is called myth, folktale, legend, fairy tale, oral poetry, ethnography. After the soldiers arrive, it is called history.
Paula Gunn Allen

How can one not speak about war, poverty, and inequality when people who suffer from these afflictions don't have a voice to speak?
Isabel Allende

No matter how big a nation is, it is no stronger that its weakest people, and as long as you keep a person down, some part of you has to be down there to hold him down, so it means you cannot soar as you might otherwise.
Marian Anderson

We cannot change the past, but we can change our attitude toward it. Uproot guilt and plant forgiveness. Tear out arrogance and seed humility. Exchange love for hate — thereby, making the present comfortable and the future promising.
Maya Angelou

Reconciliation should be accompanied by justice, otherwise it will not last. While we all hope for peace it shouldn't be peace at any cost but peace based on principle, on justice.
Corazon Aquino

The sad truth is that most evil is done by people who never make up their minds to be good or evil.
Hannah Arendt

Hungry people cannot be good at learning or producing anything, except perhaps violence.
Pearl Bailey

The shepherd always tries to persuade the sheep that their interests and his own are the same.
Marie Beyle

To eat bread without hope is still slowly to starve to death.
Pearl S. Buck

If we learn to open our hearts, anyone, including the people who drive us crazy, can be our teacher.
Pema Chodron

Courage is like — it's a habitus, a habit, a virtue: you get it by courageous acts. It's like you learn to swim by swimming. You learn courage by couraging.
Mary Daly

Gandhi once declared that it was his wife who unwittingly taught him the effectiveness of non-violence. Who better than women should know that battles can be won without resort to physical strength? Who better than we should know all the power that resides in noncooperation?
Barbara Deming

So long as little children are allowed to suffer, there is no true love in this world.
Isadora Duncan

Institutionalized in sports, the military, acculturated sexuality, the history and mythology of heroism, violence is taught to boys until they become its advocates.
Andrea Dworkin

We do not have a money problem in America. We have a values and priorities problem.
Marian Wright Edelman

You cannot shake hands with a clenched fist.
Indira Gandhi

All wars are wars among thieves who are too cowardly to fight and who therefore induce the young manhood of the whole world to do the fighting for them.
Emma Goldman

If we just worry about the big picture, we are powerless. So my secret is to start right away doing whatever little work I can do. I try to give joy to one person in the morning, and remove the suffering of one person in the afternoon. If you and your friends do not despise the small work, a million people will remove a lot of suffering. That is the secret. Start right now.
Sister Chän Khöng

Security is mostly a superstition. It does not exist in nature, nor do the children of humans as a whole experience it. Avoiding danger is not safer in the long run than outright exposure. Life is either a daring adventure, or nothing.
Helen Keller

Countermovements among racists and sexists and nazifiers are just as relentless as dirt on a coffee table. . . . Every housewife knows that if you don't sooner or later dust . . . the whole place will be dirty again.
Florynce Kennedy

If you think you're too small to have an impact, try going to bed with a mosquito in the room.
Anita Roddick

If we could raise one generation with unconditional love, there would be no Hitlers. We need to teach the next generation of children from Day One that they are responsible for their lives. Mankind's greatest gift, also its greatest curse, is that we have free choice. We can make our choices built from love or from fear.
Dr. Elizabeth Kubler-Ross

Most people, no doubt, when they espouse human rights, make their own mental reservations about the proper application of the word "human."
Suzanne LaFollette

The power of the harasser, the abuser, the rapist depends above all on the silence of women.
Ursula LeGuin

Peace as a positive condition of society, not merely as an interim between wars, is something so unknown that it casts no images on the mind's screen.
Denise Levertov

Having two bathrooms ruined the capacity to cooperate.
Margaret Mead

Many oppressors are also oppressed. Nonviolent confrontation is the only confrontation that allows us to respond realistically to such complexity.
Jane Meyerding

Establishing lasting peace is the work of education; all politics can do is keep us out of war.
Maria Montessori

What one decides to do in crisis depends on one's philosophy of life, and that philosophy cannot be changed by an incident. If one hasn't any philosophy in crises, others make the decision.
Jeannette Rankin

There is nowhere you can go and only be with people who are like you. Give it up.
Bernice Johnson Reagon

I have not been animated in my life to fight against race and sex discrimination simply because of my own identity. That would mean that one must be South African to fight apartheid, or a poor white in Appalachia to fight poverty, or Jewish to fight anti-Semitism. And I just reject that conception of how struggles should be waged.
Eleanor Holmes Norton

If you're going to hold someone down you're going to have to hold on by the other end of the chain. You are confined by your own repression.
Toni Morrison

Did St. Francis really preach to the birds? Whatever for? If he really liked birds he would have done better to preach to the cats.
Rebecca West

If you are trying to transform a brutalized society into one where people can live in dignity and hope, you begin with the empowering of the most powerless. You build from the ground up.
Adrienne Rich

It's odd how those who dismiss the peace movement as utopian don't hesitate to proffer the most absurdly dreamy reasons for going to war: to stamp out terrorism, install democracy, eliminate fascism, and most entertainingly, to "rid the world of evil-doers."
Arundhati Roy

The universe is made up of stories, not atoms.
Muriel Rukeyser

When men talk about defense, they always claim to be protecting women and children, but they never ask the women and children what they think.
Pat Schroeder

The most destructive element in the human mind is fear. Fear creates aggressiveness.
Dorothy Thompson

The most important question in the world is, 'Why is the child crying?'
Alice Walker

I myself have never been able to find out precisely what feminism is; I only know that people call me a feminist whenever I express sentiments that differentiate me from a doormat or a prostitute.
Rebecca West

Facilitator's Manual for the Class of Nonviolence

NOBEL WOMEN WORD SEARCH PUZZLE

```
D G X D M B W I E Q C T P Z T R T D N E N B N J Z I F T P I
U W W A N G A R I M A A T H A I J D B S N P K S A H X S J B
S A S E R E T R E H T O M T F Y E D O A T J M L P X R N U J
C G J H S U K B J T P W J K U M B Z V R G M V Y C M A F F A
J O S L U H O O W Q C T Z Q I Z O P H E F A L H H G K A Q J
S X N F M F I U P C E U Y L G V U F Z Z M F V W I K V B D W
T W D X P U S R G O O S Y G R Z J E A Y Q E D R H W G T I X
Y U B Q A W X M I X R G S N M A A Y R Y R S R C O U H Z J J
I I U J W X Q J U N R I Z I N T V D F G W O R P U L W J Q O
I Q R M A L G K V E E W G E F D A O N L C B H Y N C D L J D
J B L D L K E W E S Z B A O K L X G C D T S Z P C Z F Z R Y
Q E M Y Y H Z N S B Y D A Y B N S M A I L L I W Y T T E B W
G R K V U J B A L D D R J D K E O E X C L M Z P K E C B Y I
Y T J K P A F D W A G G M T I N R C F Z N R H C R R I N Q L
J H N P L J U G M F S E J C T I Q T I W V P Z N C F B I C L
U A B C Q G R S E V R A U L A J D B A S V F I O K W G C V I
V V H E H F G B X X Y U D M E G D E C M S X P J M Z F L B A
R O N E I E G U W C N N T N C B H Z A A E A Z I J Q M G K M
H N X K X A G R W Z N G W P E X N M R I V N R H N S R W F S
G S Q S K H D D N W Z S F A I J A J K L E I C A D X H T I D
J U V Q O E Y M O S A A F M I D N G H L C E P H T H M R G C
L T D Y X K C B X F L N V O W I Y G L I C F Y O U W O Q T A
F T X K R F S V V R H G R K B S D O Y W W Z K A Y T A Y W T
J N C T B G K I U L L S G T E O Z P L Y M U W U V T U W R K
N E Q N J R L J A G F U A I Y J A P L T H M B L S E X M H C
H R Q I Q W O D C H J U B V Q W A L C T O I I M W O A J Q S
I O O C V G T H M H A K J B S X X I T E Q N Z G H F Q F Y C
Z I I C U W B F S X R Y I Q A I X O H B O Z A R S H R X U G
L F X W Y Z P G Y R N I H H O S W U T N Y A J Q T D A B C C
L X I L D H K P K Q J A G A O Y N H K O G J O J T C I Q U Y
```

Bertha Von Suttner (Austrian, 1905)
Her pacifist novel *Lay Down Your Arms* had great impact. Through her friendship with Alfred Nobel she influenced him to establish the Nobel Prizes. She was the first woman awarded the Peace Prize.

Jane Addams (U.S., 1931)
An American social worker, a leader in the woman's suffrage and pacifist movements.

Emily Green Balch (U.S., 1946)
An economist and sociologist, cofounder of the Women's International League for Peace and Freedom.

Betty Williams and **Mairead Corrigan**
(Northern Ireland, 1976)
Formed the Peace People Organization, a movement of Catholics and Protestants dedicated to ending sectarian fighting in Northern Ireland.

Mother Teresa (India, 1979)
Founded the Missionaries of Charity, which operates shools, hospitals, orphanages & food centers worldwide.

Alva Myrdal (Sweden, 1982)
Sociologist, diplomat and political leader; led Sweden's delegation to the UN Disarmament Conference in Geneva and was minister of disarmament and church affairs.

Aung Sang Suu Kyi (Myanmar, 1991)
Her outspoken criticism of the military leaders of Myanmar made her a symbol of popular desire for political freedom and a focus of nonviolent opposition to dictatorship.

Rigoberta Menchu Tum (Guatemala, 1992)
Worked to secure and protect the rights of indigenous peoples in her country and to promote intercultural peace.

Jody Williams (U.S., 1997)
Established the International Campaign to Ban Landmines (ICBL). In 1997, 89 nations signed an international treaty banning international landmines.

Shirin Ebadi (Iran, 2003)
Promotes the rights of women and children in her home country.

Wangari Maathai (Kenya, 2004)
An ecologist; works with women to reverse African deforestation.

Find the names of these women who have been awarded the Nobel Peace Prize hidden in the grid. Answers can be backward and on the diagonal.

Musical Interlude: Songs About Domestic Violence

Time: ½ hour
Supplies: Music and a way to play it, lyric sheets

The lyrics to these three songs are laid out on the next page. Each person should have a copy. The songs can be downloaded for 99¢ apiece from <www.itunes.com>:
 I've Got to Go Now, by Toni Childs (from album *Toni Childs Ultimate Collection*)
Behind the Wall, by Tracy Chapman (from album *Tracy Chapman*)
Black Eyes on Blue Tears, by Shania Twain (from album *Come On Over*)

Another possible song is "*Kim*," by Eminem. The lyrics <www.azlyrics.com/lyrics/eminem/kim.html> are VERY explicit and offensive, but they do introduce the abuser's perspective. Use your judgment.

These songs can be listened to and discussed as a group or, if you can swing it logistically, the conversation will go deeper if you can divide the group into three, furnish each with the music and a boom box, and have them discuss one song and present their insights to the group.

Some questions we have found useful in relating music to the readings:
    What is the TONE of the song? (Is it angry, hopeful, funny, depressing)
    Is there a line or verse that struck a chord with you? Why?
    What do you think the songwriter was trying to say?
    Do you agree with the message of this song? Why or why not?
    Does the song recall anything from the readings for this session?
    Do you know of any other songs on this topic?

Poem: Peace is a Woman

Time: 5-10 minutes
Supplies: Copy of the poem (page 95)

This moving poem can be used as an opening meditation, a closing reflection or to welcome people back after a break.

I've Got to Go Now
By Toni Childs

This man I married is buried deep
And the more I try to wake him, the more he sleeps
I used to think I knew this man
The tenderness, not the back of his hand

It's been two weeks since he last had a drink
But the time bombs ticking, I can never sleep
It would be easier if he did
Why do you stay here, stay with him?

Why do you do it?
Why do you treat us bad?
When you've got two kids that love you
And a wife that's missing you bad
I've got to go now
I've got to say goodbye
Don't try to stop us now
And please don't you cry
Can't you see. We've all been through it
It's all been said before
With all these fears,
For how many years can I keep coming
Back for more
No more

Must be addicted to all this pain
Cause I keep coming back for the shame
Dear God give me the strength to leave
I've got to keep going, keep going this time

Don't try to stop us now
Don't pull that stuff on me
I've got the kids all packed up
Harry's in the back with his pick up truck
Jenny's fallen asleep again
I've got to keep driving till I reach the end

I can't come back here anymore
And I know it, And I know it
I cant come back here anymore
And I know it, And I know it

Behind the Wall
By Tracy Chapman

Last night I heard the screaming
Loud voices behind the wall
Another sleepless night for me
It won't do no good to call
The police
Always come late
If they come at all

And when they arrive
They say they can't interfere

With domestic affairs
Between a man and his wife
And as they walk out the door
The tears well up in her eyes

Last night I heard the screaming
Then a silence that chilled my soul
I prayed that I was dreaming
When I saw the ambulance in the road

And the policeman said
I'm here to keep the peace
Will the crowd disperse?
I think we all could use some sleep

Black Eyes, Blue Tears
By Shania Twain

Black eyes, I don't need 'em
Blue tears, gimme freedom
Positively never goin' back
I won't live where things are so out of whack
No more rollin' with the punches
No more usin' or abusin'

I'd rather die standing
Than live on my knees
Begging please-no more

Black eyes-I don't need 'em
Blue tears-gimme freedom
Black eyes-all behind me
Blue tears'll never find me now

Definitely found my self esteem
Finally-I'm forever free to dream
No more cryin' in the corner
No excuses-no more bruises

I'd rather die standing
Than live on my knees
Begging please-no more

Black eyes-I don't need 'em
Blue tears-gimme freedom
Black eyes-all behind me
Blue tears'll never find me now

I'd rather die standing
Than live on my knees, begging please...

Black eyes-I don't need 'em
Blue tears-gimme freedom
Black eyes-all behind me
Blue tears'll never find me now

It's all behind me, they'll never find me now
Find your self-esteem and be forever free to dream

Reflection: Peace is a Woman Poem

Time: 5 minutes
Supplies: Copy of the poem

This sad, beautiful yet hopeful poem would make a fitting reflection at the beginning or the end of your lesson. Read it aloud: one person could read the first stanza, another the second. Read it slowly. Read it again. Give everyone a copy to take home. Read it every day. Read it to your mother. Read it for all the mothers. Just read it.

Peace Is A Woman And A Mother
by Ada Ahroni

How do you know peace is a woman?
I know, for I met her yesterday
on my winding way to the world's fare.
She had such a sorrowful face
just like a golden flower faded
before her prime.
I asked her why she was so sad?
She told me her baby was killed in Auschwitz,
her daughter in Hiroshima, and her sons in Vietnam,
Ireland, Israel, Palestine, Lebanon, Rwanda,
Bosnia, Kosovo and Chechnya...

All the rest of her children, she said,
are on the nuclear black-list of the dead,
all the rest, unless the whole world understands –
that peace is a woman.
A thousand candles then lit
in her starry eyes, and I saw cherubim
bearing a moonlit message:
Peace is indeed a pregnant woman -
Peace is a mother.

Discussion Topic: Power

Time: 10-20 minutes
Supplies: whiteboard or big paper

At this point it is useful to clarify what the class understands about the term "power." Is power a good thing, a bad thing or a neutral thing? Is power always dominating (power over) or is there such as thing as "power with," when we cooperate with others to achieve shared ends? Or "power-from-within," inner strength associated with courage, conviction, creativity and self-discipline? Can you recall a time you felt powerful? Felt powerless? Must power corrupt? What does power have to do with nonviolence?

These definitions of power could be a conversational starting point:
In physics: the amount of work done or energy transferred per unit of time; *motive power* is the power which moves something.
In sociology: the ability to make choices or influence outcomes.
In politics: the ability to influence the behavior of others.
In philosophy: the cause of the spread of a set of ideas.

It could also be useful to discuss some of the sources of power, for example:
Reward power: control over valued resources.
Coercive power: ability to inflict punishment, possibly physical.
Expert power: superior knowledge.
Legitimate power: formal rank or position.
Referent power: when people want to be like you.

Kenneth Boulding, in his theory of power, says power has three forms: **threat, exchange and love** (also called destructive power, productive power and integrative power.) Threat power is equivalent to "power over." Exchange power is the power of negotiation—it is a form of "power with," as it requires another party to negotiate with. Love, Boulding argued, is also a form of power. Although not often recognized as power, when people love each other, they do things to help the other person, just because they love them, not for any particular reward or hope of exchange. This gives rise to what Boulding calls "the integrative system"—the structure of bonds, of respect, of legitimacy that holds social groups and whole societies together.

Another interesting theory about power that applies particularly well to this session on feminism, peace and power is that of the "**unmarked category**."

According to this theory, the powerful are those who can gain ready access to power and are able to exercise it without thinking about what they are doing. For the powerful the culture is obvious, accessible and made just for them. For the powerless it is unreachable, impenetrable, elite and expensive. The 'unmarked category' is the identifying mark of the powerful: he is the standard by which everything else is measured.

Whiteness is not visible to the powerful, because they themselves are white. Whiteness, to the white, is normal and he cannot recognize white privilege. It has a normative status in the same way that 'man' has a normative status. What other 'unmarked categories' exist? How is this reflected in our society?

(Susan sometimes tells this real-life story of "Christian" being the "unmarked category." At an interfaith prayer service the next song to be sung was "Amazing Grace." It's generally accepted to sing an explicitly Christian song such as this one in an interfaith service as long as music from other faiths is also included. However, the pastor/emcee blew it when he commented ". . . and since everyone knows the words to this one we don't even need to open our hymnals." Everyone? When was the last time they sang "Amazing Grace" in a mosque or temple? In that one sentence "Christian" became the norm and everything else a deviation from the norm.)

Exercise: Violence Wheel and Nonviolence Wheels
Time: 10 – 30 minutes
Supplies: A copy of the wheels for everyone

The violence and nonviolence wheels (reproduced on the next two pages) were developed by the Domestic Abuse Intervention Project — Duluth, Minnesota and are widely used to demonstrate how physical and sexual violence are fed by actions that arise from the desire for power and control while, conversely, nonviolence in relationships revolve around actions and attitudes that radiate from equality.

The most engaging way to use these wheels is to draw a blank "power over" wheel on a chalkboard or flip chart. Include the headings (such as "using intimidation") but do not include the subsequent text. Have the class brainstorm to come up with examples for each category, prompting with examples from the complete wheel when necessary. Do the same for the "power with" wheel. (The original wheels were called "power and control" and "equality." We took the liberty of changing them to "Power over" and "Power with.")

We've put copies of the partially-completed wheels on this book's Website, at <www/salsa.net/peace/ebooks/fmconv>. You can use these as handouts if drawing blank wheels on the board is inconvenient.

Make sure everyone get copies of the compete wheels to keep.

This wheel format is also useful for analyzing *any* relationships and societal structures that are based on power and control, such as some worker-employer relationships, or those with immigrants, the poor, homeless, minorities, children and those with disabilities.

Facilitator's Manual for the Class of Nonviolence

VIOLENCE

physical · **sexual**

USING COERCION AND THREATS
Making and/or carrying out threats to do something to hurt her * threatening to leave her, to commit suicide, to report her to welfare * Making her drop charges * Making her do illegal things

USING INTIMIDATION
Making her afraid by using looks, actions, gestures * smashing things * destroying her property - abusing pets * displaying weapons

USING ECONOMIC ABUSE
Preventing her from getting or keeping a job * making her ask for money- giving her an allowance *taking her money *not letting her know about or have access to the family income.

USING EMOTIONAL ABUSE
Putting her down making her feel bad about herself * calling her names * making her think she's crazy * playing mind games * humiliating her * making her feel guilty.

POWER OVER

MINIMIZING, DENYING & BLAMING
Making light of the abuse and not taking her concerns seriously * saying the abuse didn't happen * shifting responsibility for abusive behavior * saying she caused it

USING ISOLATION
Controlling what she does, who she sees and talks to, what she reads, where she goes * limiting her outside involvement * using jealosy to justify actions.

USING CHILDREN
Making her feel guilty about the children *using children to relay messages *using visitation to harass her *threatening to take the children away.

USING MALE PRIVILEGE
Treating her like a servant *making all the big decisions *acting like the "master of the castle" * being the one to defend men's and women's roles.

physical · **sexual** · **VIOLENCE**

NONVIOLENCE

NEGOTIATION & FAIRNESS
Seeking mutually satisfying resolutions to conflict *accepting change *being willing to compromise.

NON-THREATENING BEHAVIOR
Taling and acting so that she feels safe and comfortable expressing herself and doing things.

ECONOMIC PARTNERSHIP
Making money decisions together *making sure both partners benefit from financial arrangements.

RESPECT
Listening to her non-judgementally *being emotionally affirming and understanding *valuing opinions.

POWER WITH

HONESTY & ACCOUNTABILITY
Accepting responsibility for self *acknowledging past use of violence *admitting being wrong *communicating openly and truthfully.

TRUST & SUPPORT
Supporting her goals in life *respecting her right to her own feelings, friends, activities and opinions.

RESPONSIBLE PARENTING
Sharing parental responsibilities *being a positive nonviolent role model for the children.

SHARED RESPONSIBILITY
Mutually agreeing on a fair distribution of work *making family decisions together.

NONVIOLENCE

Exercise: Men, Women and Ardhanarishvara

Time: 15-20 minutes
Supplies: picture of Ardhanarishvara (next page**)**

The first question Colman McCarthy asks in this session is: "*Given the chance, are women just as prone to violence as men? Is it beyond men's capacity to establish a peaceful world? Are women's views of peace different from men; after all, don't women expect men to "protect" them at all costs?*"

Hindus believe in two forces in the universe: *siva,* the masculine energy, which is passive, pure consciousness and *shakti*, the feminine energy, which is the active, dynamic force that stimulates all movement and change in the universe. Both are needed for the creation, preservation, and destruction of the universe. *Ardhanarishvara*, a Hindu deity who is half male and half female, can be a springboard to discuss Colman's provocative question and reinforce that we *all* have "masculine" and "feminine" energies.

Pay particular attention to the hand gestures, or "*mudras*" in the illustration. They recall what the late writer and activist Barbara Deming wrote about the "two hands of nonviolence" in her book *Revolution and Equilibrium*: "With one hand we say to one who is angry, or to an oppressor, or to an unjust system, 'Stop what you are doing. I refuse to honor the role you are choosing to play, I refuse to obey you, I refuse to cooperate with your demands, I refuse to build the walls and the bombs. I refuse to pay for the guns. With this hand I will even interfere with the wrong you are doing. I want to disrupt the easy pattern of your life.' But then the advocate of nonviolence raises the other hand. It is raised outstretched — maybe with love and sympathy, maybe not — but always outstretched . . . With this hand we say, 'I won't let go of you or cast you out of the human race. I have faith that you can make a better choice than you are making now, and I'll be here when you are ready. Like it or not, we are part of one another.'"

The *varada mudra*, the gesture being made by the female half, symbolizes charity, compassion and boon-granting. It is the *mudra* of the accomplishment of the wish to devote oneself to human salvation. It is nearly always made with the left hand, and can be made with the arm hanging naturally at the side of the body, the palm of the open hand facing forward, and the fingers extended. The five extended fingers in this *mudra* symbolize the following five perfections: Generosity, Morality, Patience, Effort and Meditative concentration.

Abhaya, the *mudra* being made by the male half, means fearlessness in Sanskrit. Thus this *mudra* symbolizes protection, peace, and the dispelling of fear. It is made with the right hand raised to shoulder height, the arm crooked, the palm of the hand facing outward, and the fingers upright and joined. The left hand hangs down at the side of the body. This *mudra* was probably used from prehistoric times as a sign of good intentions - the hand raised and unarmed proposes friendship, or at least peace; since antiquity, it was also a gesture asserting power, as with the *magna manus* ("all powerful hand") of the Roman Emperors who legislated and gave peace at the same time.

Representations of *Ardhanarishvara* can have eight arms (or more.) What hand gestures would a peacemaking male/female make? What symbols might they hold (in the illustration the male half holds a trident and a drum; the female half holds a lotus – sometimes she is shown with a mirror.)

Art Exercise: Mother's PEACE Day Cards

Time: 20 minutes
Supplies: Cardstock, art supplies (crayons, markers, scissors, glue, etc.)

Julia Ward Howe (1819-1910) was a writer, poet, reformer and lecturer who worked throughout her life for justice. In 1861 she wrote *The Battle Hymn of the Republic* as an inspiration to Union soldiers fighting against slavery. (Hear her words about peace and justice: "*He is trampling out the vintage where the grapes of wrath are stored*" and "*As he died to make men holy, let us live to make men free.*")

She founded, with Lucy Stone and others, the New England Women's Club, which later became the American Woman Suffrage Association. She lectured, wrote and lobbied not only for the right to vote, but also to liberate women from the confinement of the traditional "woman's place" in stifling marriages like her own, where none of her ideas were valued or accepted. She also worked for world peace, founding, in 1891, the American Friends of Russian Freedom, and serving as president, in 1894, of the United Friends of Armenia.

During the U.S. Civil War she was a nurse. In 1872, horrified by the atrocities committed by both sides the Franco-Prussan War, Howe proposed a "Mother's Day." Let her speak for herself: the proclamation and a reflection she wrote to explain her intent are on the following page.

Although it gained international circulation and acclaim, he idea was not realized in her lifetime. Mother's Day, as we know it, was proclaimed by President Woodrow Wilson in 1914, based on a campaign initiated by Ana Jarvis of Philadelphia. It didn't turn out as expected. Enraged by the commercialization of the holiday, Jarvis filed a lawsuit to stop a 1923 Mother's Day festival and was arrested for disturbing the peace at a war mothers' convention where women sold white carnations — Jarvis' symbol for mothers — to raise money.

Mothers throughout the country still remember Julia Ward Howe's original vision for a Mother's Peace Day. In Arizona, for example, the campaign for a U.S. Department of Peace delivers apple pies to the congressional representatives on Mother's Day with the message "Peace Deserves a Piece of the Pie."

So here's the project (finally!): Have the class — as individuals or small groups of two or three — design mother's peace day cards. Use Julia Ward Howe's words, phrases taken from the readings or original text and images. Don't worry if you're not an artist - it's the concept that counts. Share your cards.

Julia Ward Howe's
Mother's Day Proclamation, 1872

Arise, then, women of this day!

Arise all women who have hearts, whether your baptism be that of water or of fears!

Say firmly: "We will not have great questions decided by irrelevant agencies.

Our husbands shall not come to us reeking with carnage, for caresses and applause.

Our sons shall not be taken from us to unlearn all that we have been able to teach them of charity, mercy, and patience.

We women of one country will be too tender of those of another country to allow our sons to be trained to injure theirs.

From the bosom of the devastated earth a voice goes up with our own. It says, "Disarm, Disarm!"

The sword of murder is not the balance of justice! Blood does not wipe out dishonor nor violence indicate possession.

As men have often forsaken the plow and the anvil at the summons of war, let women now leave all that may be left of home for a great and earnest day of counsel.

Let them meet first, as women, to bewail and commemorate the dead.

Let them then solemnly take counsel with each other as the means whereby the great human family can live in peace,

And each bearing after her own time the sacred impress, not of Caesar, but of God.

The origins of Julia Ward Howe's Mother's Day Proclamation

(from Julia Ward Howe, REMINISCENCES, 1819-1899, (Boston, Houghton, Mifflin and Co., 1899); pp 327-329)

As I was revolving these matters in my mind, while the war* was still in progress, I was visited by a sudden feeling of the cruel and unnecessary character of the contest. It seemed to me a return to barbarism, the issue having been one which might easily have been settled without bloodshed. The question forced itself upon me, "Why do not the mothers of mankind interfere in these matters, to prevent the waste of that human life of which they alone bear and know the cost?" I had never thought of this before. The august dignity of motherhood and its terrible responsibilities now appeared to me in a new aspect, and I could think of no better way of expressing my sense of these than that of sending forth an appeal to womanhood throughout the world, which I then and there composed. I did not dare to make this public without the advice of some wise counselor, and sought such an one in the person of Rev. Charles T. Brooks of Newport, a beloved friend and esteemed pastor.

The little document which I drew up in the heat of my enthusiasms implored woman, all the world over, to awake to the knowledge of the sacred right vested in them as mothers to protect the human life which costs them so many pangs. I did not doubt but that my appeal would find a ready response in the hearts of great numbers of women throughout the limits of civilization. I invited these imagined helpers to assist me in calling and holding a congress of women in London, and at once began a wide task of correspondence for the realization of this plan. My first act was to have my appeal translated into various languages, to wit: French, Spanish, Italian, German, and Swedish, and to distribute copies of it as widely as possible. I devoted the next two years almost entirely to correspondence with leading women in various countries. I also had two important meetings in New York, at which the cause of peace and the ability of women to promote it were earnestly presented. At the first of these, which took place in the late autumn of 1870, Mr. [William Cullen] Bryant gave me his venerable presence and valuable words. At the second, in the spring following, David Dudley Field, an eminent member of the New York bar, and a lifelong advocate of international arbitration, made a very eloquent and convincing address.

* Howe is referring to the Franco-Prussian War between France and Germany, 1870-1871.

Facilitator's Manual for the Class of Nonviolence

"In 1989, thirteen nations comprising 1,695,000 people experienced nonviolent revolutions that succeeded beyond anyone's wildest expectations . . . If we add all the countries touched by major nonviolent actions in our century (the Philippines, South Africa . . . the independence movement in India . . .) the figure reaches 3,337,400,000, a staggering 65% of humanity! All this in the teeth of the assertion, endlessly repeated, that nonviolence doesn't work in the 'real' worl"
Walter Wink

Class of Nonviolence
Lesson 6
Nonviolence Works!

Essays for Lesson Six

The Technique of Nonviolent Action by Gene Sharp
The Politics of Nonviolent Action by Gene Sharp
The Methods of Nonviolent Protest and Persuasion by Gene Sharp
Albert Einstein on Pacifism
Letter to Ernesto Cardenal: Guns Don't Work by Daniel Berrigan
Building Confidence at Prairie Creek by Colman McCarthy

Questions for Lesson Six

Explain how the concept of satyagraha
applies to Poland's resistance to the Soviet Union.

Many believe that Britain could have been removed from
America nonviolently. Explain.

If "guns don't work" as Daniel Berrigan asserts,
why do humans keep resorting to them to resolve conflict?

Explain why pacifism is an active a
and not a passive approach to conflict resolution.

Research and report on a creative demonstration
of nonviolent conflict resolution.

Who are the authors for this session?

Gene Sharp: is a political scientist, author and founder of the Albert Einstein Institution, a nonprofit organization which studies and promotes the use of nonviolent action.
Albert Einstein: was the recipient of the Nobel Prize in Physics and a pacifist.
Daniel Berrigan: is a Jesuit priest and an internationally renowned poet and American peace activist. Daniel and his brother Philip performed non-violent actions against war and were for a time on the FBI Ten Most Wanted Fugitives list.
Ernesto Cardenal: is a Trappist priest and was one of the most famous liberation theologians of the Nicaraguan Revolution. He is also famous as a poet, and was the founder of the primitivist art community in the Solentiname Islands.

About this session, and the next one:
We do a little shuffling to sharpen the focus of sessions six and seven. In this session we focus on "nonviolence works," while in the next session, seven, we divide our time between civil disobedience and war. We therefore switch question 3 from session seven to this one (*Explain how the concept of satyagraha applies to Poland's resistance to the Soviet Union*) and postpone question 1 from this session until next week (*The principle of a "just war" is merely the clever dodge of a government bent on violence. Explain.*)

Display/Altar
We generally use cards from the "Great Peace March" (see a description on page 113) as our display/altar material. A world map or globe would be appropriate, symbolizing the global reach — success!— of nonviolence. Ask each person to bring something that reflects the readings: a piece of the Berlin Wall; a t-shirt, button, yard sign, poster or bumper sticker from a past or current nonviolent campaign; or a photo of a nonviolent action or activist downloaded from the Internet or copied from a book.

Films for this Session:

The ideal film for this session is "**A Force More Powerful**" <www.aforcemorepowerful.com>. Any of the 25-minute episodes will do, but we have found that the "Denmark" episode is good at debunking the assumption that World War II was a good and necessary war, one in which nonviolence would not have worked.

> **South Africa**-Freedom In Our Lifetime: Young activist Mkhuseli Jack leads a consumer boycott campaign against apartheid in the black townships of the Eastern Cape Province of South Africa.

> **Denmark**-Living With The Enemy: During five years of Nazi occupation, Danes' noncooperation undermines the Germans' attempt to exploit Denmark for food and war materiel, and rescues all but a few hundred of Denmark's seven thousand Jews from the Holocaust.

> **Poland**-We've Caught God by the Arm: The 1980 Gdansk Shipyard strike wins Poles the right to have free trade unions, launches the Solidarity movement, and catapults him to national labor leader and eventually president of Poland.

> **Chile**-Defeat Of A Dictator: Overcoming a decade of paralyzing fear, Chilean copper miners trigger a national day of protest of the dictatorship of Gen. Augusto Pinochet, leading to years of nonviolent organizing and culminating in victory in a plebiscite to end his rule.

Meditation: Berrigan and Cardenal poems

Time: 10 minutes
Supplies: copy of poems (following page)

Both Daniel Berrigan and Ernesto Cardenal (the fifth essay in this section) are poets.
There is a free 2-minute video of Ernesto Cardenal reading his poem "*Psalm 5*" at <www.prolefeedstudios.com/catalog/psalm5/psalm5.html> which can be downloaded for later showing on a computer. Even without the video clip, a reading of Cardenal's "*Psalm 5*" would make a moving introduction to the reading, along with a poem (such as "*Accounts Come Home*") from Fr. Berrigan. We included both on the next page.

PSALM 5—A Paraphrase
Ernesto Cardenal

HEAR MY PROTEST
Hear my words, Oh Lord,
give ear to my groanings.
Listen to my protest.
For you are not a God
who is friendly with oppressors,
nor do you support their devious ways,
nor are you influenced by their propaganda,
nor are you a cohort with gangsters.
One cannot believe anything they say,
nor have any confidence
in their official pronouncements.
They talk of peace
while they increase their production of arms.
They make gestures toward understanding
at the Peace Conferences,
but in secret they prepare for war.
. . . .
Punish them, Oh God,
bring to naught their machinations.

Accounts Come Home
by Daniel Berrigan, sj

Taking in account all kinds of things
from the state of the economy

to the state of the union
to the state of amnesia

which like 50 or more states
(kids can name them)

is like a gang rape
in a swedish nursery
or a fire drill in hell —

will someone please inform me
precisely when
we died

or why that
departure, arrival
is

by recorded announcement
put off
and off
and off
Having no tears like
having no money

O where shall I replenish
the springs of my eyes?

The children ring me round
tin cups in dead hands
clamoring —

'O give me tears

you stole our blood
to make your bread

spun us blindfold
in a game you great ones

we whirl we topple
it's like death except
for death they weep

but for us
no one knows
no one
knows
no
one
knows

Question: American Revolution

Time: 20-40 minutes

Supplies: Copy of the audio book version of "*Nonviolence: 25 Lessons from the History of a Dangerous Idea*," by Mark Kurlansky and/or copies of *Disregarded History: The Power of Nonviolent Action* by Gene Sharp (pages 110-112, following)

One of the questions that Colman McCarthy poses for this session is: "*Many believe that Britain could have been removed from America nonviolently. Explain.*"

The obvious answer is that the American "colonials" could have used many of the same techniques that Gandhi used more than a century later. To get past this fuzzy notion, however, requires a depth of knowledge about American history most of our students have been lacking: understandable, given the narrow way history is taught in our schools.

But we're in luck! Mark Kurlansky, in his book "*Nonviolence: 25 Lessons from the History of a Dangerous Idea*" (2007: Modern Library) covers the nonviolent prelude to the American Revolution in chapter VI: Natural Revolution.

We bought the audio book (<www.recordedbooks.com>; narrated by Richard Dreyfus.) Chapter VI is covered in disk three, 3k to 3s (or tracks 11-19, depending on how your CD player works.) It is eleven pages, just over a half hour of audio. It is well worth listening to as a group as background to the question.

If you can't spare the time to play the CD, consider asking the week before if one or several of the class participants will volunteer to research this question. In addition to Kurlansky's book, other sources include:

"*The Real Revolution: The Global Story of American Independence*" (2005: Clarion) by Marc Aronson, which ties the American Revolution in to global movements, including, appropriately for this question, those in India at the time. This young adult book is well worth reading.

"*People's History of the United States*" by Howard Zinn (2005: Harper)

"*A People's History of the American Revolution*" (2001: Perennial) by Ray Raphael.

Have them report back to the class. Another alternative is to use Gene Sharp's excellent article, reproduced on the following three pages: read it during class, or hand it out the week before as an addition to the readings.

Disregarded History
The Power of Nonviolent Action
By Gene Sharp

Extracted from an article originally published in the March 1976 issue of Fellowship magazine.

American Colonial Nonviolence, Circa 1776

In the 18th century, here in this part of North America, the European settlers used a great deal of violence against indigenous Americans, and then against the Africans who were imported. Nevertheless, the European settlers conducted major campaigns of nonviolent struggle against English controls, particularly for the ten-year period from 1765 to 1775. This was on a scale and significance that may require, when it is more fully researched, a major reinterpretation of American history, which may lead to a reassessment of the relevance and importance of the War of Independence.

There were three separate campaigns, each of which involved economic resistance. It is possible that this is the first major case of international economic sanctions on record.

Daniel Dulany, in the pamphlet he wrote on resistance to the Stamp Act in October of 1765, describes certain basic characteristics of political nonviolent struggle. (Now you'll notice I'm discussing on the political level, not on the religious or moral level.) Dulany said, *"Instead of moping and whining to excite compassion, in such a situation we ought with spirit and vigor and alacrity to bid defiance to tyranny by exposing its impotence, by making it as contemptible as it would be detestable."* Here is the fundamental conception that you can make tyranny helpless by refusing cooperation with it. So he advocated building up economic production within the colonies to make them self-reliant. They could then sever trade relations with England, which would hurt the English merchants, and consequently this would put leverage on the English government to repeal the Stamp Act.

George Washington, Nonviolent Strategist

Did you ever think of George Washington as a nonviolent strategist? During this Stamp Act struggle courts were required to use stamps on official documents. The colonists had decided not to use the stamps. So the question became: *"Do the courts remain open without using the stamps, or do the courts close down?"* This was in the context of colonists conducting a massive campaign to refuse to pay debts they owed to the English merchants from whom the colonial merchants had purchased their products on credit. Walpole regarded this as the most effective weapon that the colonists wielded. So George Washington advised that they should close down the courts, of course. Obeying the law was impossible. You close the courts, Washington reasoned, because if you close the courts, the courts cannot be used in an effort to collect the money that the colonists were refusing to pay to the English merchants. Therefore, the English merchants would put pressure on their government to repeal the Stamp Act. Very sophisticated nonviolent strategy, calculating effects and counter-effects of specific types of non-cooperation.

Thomas Jefferson, Faster

Did you know that Thomas Jefferson with his colleagues introduced fasting in the colonial struggle? When the spirit of the resistance was weakening at certain points and people were getting bored, he and his friends (who were known rather as playboys, always going out and dancing) got the very respected and staid chaplain of the Virginia House of Burgesses to propose as his own idea a day of fasting and prayer—for political resistance. It was passed by the House of Burgesses and all of Virginia had a day of fasting and prayer—for political resistance. It wasn't Gandhi who introduced fasting as a political weapon at all.

Later during 1765, Governor Bernard of Massachusetts Bay said: "*At this time I have no real authority in this place.*" And Lieutenant Governor Thomas Hutchinson of Massachusetts Bay said: "*In the capital towns of several of the colonies and of this in particular, the authority is in the populace. No law can be carried into execution against their minds.*" There were cases—significant cases—of the burning of buildings and destruction of property during the Stamp Act resistance. Men who had accepted appointments as stamp distributors were threatened with physical attack and even death and run out of town. But not one person was killed.

During the Townshend resistance in January 1769, a London newspaper reported that because of the refusal of taxes and the refusal to import British goods, only 3,500 pounds sterling of revenue had been produced in the colonies. The American non-importation and non-consumption campaign was estimated by the same newspaper at that point to have cost British business not a mere 3,500 pounds but 7,250,000 pounds in lost income. Those figures may not have been accurate, but they are significant of the perceptions of the time. The attempt to collect the tax against that kind of opposition was not worth the effort, and the futility of trying eventually became apparent.

As the American movement developed, a radical fringe began to talk the rhetoric of violence. The militias, which the colonies had had for many, many decades, were deliberately developed. Some people began to foresee the movement shifting over to war. But this was not universal, and not preferred by even many radicals. The Suffolk Resolves, passed by the delegates of Suffolk County of Massachusetts Bay in 1774, recognized that violence was possible and the colonists should be ready for violence if it came. However, they recommended instead a different type of struggle—like they had been using: "*We would heartily recommend to all persons of this community not to engage in any routs, riots or licentious attacks upon the properties of any persons whatsoever, as being subversive of all order and government; but, by a steady, manly, uniform, and persevering opposition, to convince our enemies that in a contest so important—in a cause so solemn, our conduct shall be such as to merit the approbation of the wise, and the admiration of the brave and free of every age and of every country.*"

On the basis of such thought and the Virginia Association, the First Continental Congress developed a sophisticated, phased program of economic and political non-cooperation. First, it began with a non-importation campaign, to be followed, if necessary, by a non-exportation campaign. The First Continental Congress program of resistance was called the "Continental Association." It was a program of nonviolent resistance and the First Continental Congress was a nonviolent resistance organization. It was a program implemented throughout the colonies, so well developed, so sophisticated, that its equal was probably not seen until Gandhi's work in India. Going along with this was a program of enforcement of these provisions in the colonies with such complete solidarity that the very enforcement organizations in many cases gradually became instruments of local government. Development of parallel governmental institutions also occurred on a colony-wide basis, sometimes in deliberate defiance of British-appointed governors. It has been estimated that in nine or ten of the thirteen colonies, British governmental power had already been effectively and illegally replaced by substitute governments before Lexington and Concord. The Continental Congress was known as "the Congress." Its measures of resistance were known as "laws." British power had de facto collapsed in most of the colonies before a shot was fired. In Maryland, for example, an entire substitute government had taken over.

At the same time, there was significant support in England for the movement (though not as strong as during the Stamp Act resistance). The extent of the support, and the reasoning for it, should be researched and analyzed. Part of the Continental Association (the program of resistance of the Continental Congress) contained this phrase: "...we are of the opinion that a non-importation, non-consumption and non-exportation agreement, faithfully adhered to, will prove the most speedy, effectual, and peaceable measure..."

Considering the de facto independence of most of the colonies by 1775, with the emergence of an inter-colonial confederation-type of government, and the experience in the Stamp Act struggles and the Townshend resistance, it is very possible that British power might have totally collapsed *de jure* short of the eight years that it took for the War of Independence. Rather than the war having speeded up independence, it may very well have postponed it.

Governor Dunmore of Virginia suggested that the "laws of Congress," as he put it, receive from Virginians *Marks of reverence they never bestowed on their legal Government, or the laws proceeding from it."* He added: *"I have discovered no incidence where the interposition of Government, in the feeble state to which it is reduced, could serve any other purpose than to suffer the disgrace of a disappointment, and thereby afford matter of great exultation to its enemies and increase their influence over the minds of the people."*

And in Massachusetts, already in early 1774, the Governor—Governor Gage—wrote, *"All legislative, as well as all executive power, is gone..."* Governor Gage made a similar report later in the year. So we must remember that, disregarded as it is in present portrayals of America's Revolution, the American colonials, too, have a highly important place in the history of nonviolent struggle.

The Great Peace March

In the late 1980s the Lutheran Peace Fellowship created the "Wall of Hope," a timeline of peace and justice events that they have used in more than 500 events (look under "Peace Ed" at <www.lutheranpeace.org>). Over the years the peaceCENTER has played around with the Wall. We call it "The Great Peace March" and have added to it, illustrated it, put it into slide shows and even made up games using it. Our current Peace March has 106 events, starting with the Hebrew Midwives in 1350 BCE right up to the present day.

We have an illustrated version (4 events to a page, 27 pages) of the Great Peace March available for FREE download from a link at <www.salsa.net/peace/timeline/index.html>. It's a large PDF file (2.3 MB). We recommend printing it on white cardstock and, if you think you'll be using it more than once or twice, having it laminated (in the long run it cheaper than repeated color printing.) Each 8 ½x 11" sheet gets cut into four cards.

Exercise: History is in front of us

Time: about 10 minutes
Supplies: Great Peace March cards

When we talk about history we often use expressions such as "oh, that's all behind us now" or dismiss something as unimportant by calling it "ancient history." That's not true. History is not behind us. History is in front of us. We follow in the footsteps of those who have gone before. Just as Tolstoy followed Thoreau and Gandhi followed Tolstoy and King followed Gandhi and Chavez follow King . . . we follow in their footsteps and, someday, people will follow us! We are tomorrow's history, blazing a path for our children's children.

This exercise facilitates a discussion about events in peace and justice history while reinforcing that we are following in the footsteps of the peacemakers who have gone before us. It works best with a larger group—it doesn't make much sense with fewer than 15 people—and you can go up to 106, the number of cards. If you're dealing with a smallish group it's best to pre-select the cards you'll hand out to make sure you're covering all the important bases (make sure you include the Hebrew Midwives, early Christians, Gandhi, Thoreau, King, Chavez, etc.)

Hand everyone a card and briefly explain the concept of following in the footsteps of those who have gone before. Then, ask everyone to line up in chronological order, starting with the Hebrew Midwives. They will have to talk amongst each other and look at each other's cards to sort themselves out.

After everyone is lined up, ask them to introduce their person/event to the person in front of them and in back of them. Is it conceivable that the person or people involved in the event met in person? Could they have known about each other? (For example, George Washington (1783), Miguel Hidalgo (1810) and Lord Byron (1812) *might* have met; all three of them, as educated men, would have known about the "perpetual peace" promised at the marriage (1420) of England's Henry V and Catherine of Valois more than 400 years before their time.)

If there's time, ask every one to read their card, from first to last – the verbal timeline helps put things into historical context.

Exercise: Peace Loteria

Time: 10-20 minutes
Supplies: Great Peace March and Loteria cards; markers (beans, candy) prizes (optional)

In addition to the Great Peace March Cards (described above) you will need a Loteria card for each person. Forty cards (all different!) can be downloaded from the peaceCENTER Web site, at <www.salsa.net/peace/timeline/index.html>. As with the Great Peace March cards, print them on white cardstock; it pays to laminate them if you think you will use them more than once or twice. There are 20 pages; each page gets cut in half to make two cards. If you have more than 40 people you can have two people share a card. You will also need something to mark the completed squares: traditionally, dried pinto beans are used as markers but you can also use pennies, mints – anything about that size and affordable in quantity (you need 4 or 5 markers for each person.) If you've laminated the cards you can give each person a crayon and a tissue and wipe them down after each round.

Loteria is a Mexican game of chance, similar to Bingo, but using images on a deck of cards instead of numbered balls. You play this game just like Bingo: the caller (called the *cancionero*, or singer, in Mexico) draws a card, reads it out and when people have that event on their card, they mark it. Shuffle the cards: don't read them in chronological order.

The first person to make the designated pattern wins. Typical patterns are three in a row, an X or the four corners. Have winners call out something like "satyagraha" or "peace" instead of Bingo. Keep it moving briskly, and play three or four rounds (the bigger the group, the shorter the rounds.) Small prizes make it more exciting: a bumper sticker, a button, a piece of candy. Much to our astonishment, we've had elementary school students play this for HOURS and adults have fun with it too. Have the winner of the last game be the caller for the next one; he or she can pick the designated pattern and the "win-word" that people shout out.

Exercise: 198 Methods of Nonviolent Action

Time: about 25 minutes

Supplies: Great Peace March Cards, a copy of Gene Sharp's 198 methods of nonviolent action (download from <www.aeinstein.org/organizations/org/198_methods.pdf>), a dictionary (optional but useful), pencils and paper.

These methods were compiled by Dr. Gene Sharp and first published in his 1973 book, *The Politics of Nonviolent Action, Vol. 2: The Methods of Nonviolent Action*. (Boston: Porter Sargent Publishers, 1973). The book outlines each method and gives information about its historical use. There is an excerpt in the third essay in this session. This exercise helps people become more comfortable with his typography.

Tape the Great Peace March cards to the wall so that everyone has access to all of them (the peaceCENTER built a portable display stand out of PVC pipe; instructions are online at <www.salsa.net/peace/timeline/index.html>)

This exercise works best if you divide the class into groups of 2-4 people so that they can work as a team. Each group needs a copy of the 198 methods.

Explain that each team will try to categorize as many of the events in the Great Peace March according to Sharp's typology as they can in 10 minutes. It helps to give an example: there's a 2003 card demonstrating *Lysitradic Nonaction* (#57.) Some of the events might fit into more than one category. Make it clear that categorizing these events is a matter of art, not science: groups might come up with different answers and they may all be right. Sharp's language is a bit academic, hence the recommendation of a dictionary.

Give each group about five minutes to become familiar with the layout and content of the list and organize themselves (they might have one person manage the list, another one act as secretary and two running back and forth with events to look up.)

Then have them go at it. It should be hectic. At the end of 10 minutes call a halt and see which groups were able to categorize the most events. Give them a standing ovation. Ask each group to describe one event that they were able to categorize. Open it up for discussion.

Time saver: If you can't spare the time, don't have the space or want to avoid the chaos, an alternative is to give everyone (or divide them into pairs so they can collaborate) one or two of the Peace Loteria cards and a copy of Gene Sharp's 198 methods. Give 10 minutes for everyone to categorize as many events on their cards as they can, and then share the results with the group.

Exercise: World Backrub

Time: 5-10 minutes
Supplies: None

We often end peaceCENTER skillshops with this exercise. It fits in well at the end of this session or the next one, whenever you are talking about trouble spots in the world. It gives people a chance to express their concerns and relieve tension in a very physical way.

Have everyone stand in a circle, facing each other's backs. Explain that we are to envision the person's back in front of us as a map of the world and that we are going to give the world a backrub to ease its tensions. Help people orient themselves – start with Alaska, the left shoulder, then move over to Russia – the right shoulder, then south through Mongolia, to China, through Nepal to India. The lower back is Africa; the upper back Europe. (We sometimes set appropriate limits by pointing out that Antarctica is off limits, if the groups seems like it needs that warning.)

Model a response, such as "Everyone massage sub-Sahara Africa to find healing for the AIDS epidemic and while we're there, put some extra pressure on Darfur, to heal the wounds of genocide." Ask if anyone else knows of a place that needs healing. If no one else does so, make sure to include your own city, state, country. Keep going until the group runs out of steam. End the exercise by asking the class to give the entire world a brisk backrub.

Exercise: Upside-down World

Time: 5 minutes
Supplies: A map of the world, hung upside-down

Maps are, to a certain extent, arbitrary. From space, what do "north" and "south" mean? Nothing! The orientation of our maps do, however, shape our perspective of what nations and people are on "top." Hang a world map on the wall upside-down and initiate a brief discussion about our world view.

Facilitator's Manual for the Class of Nonviolence

Exercise: Universal Declaration of Human Rights

Time: 20-30 minutes

Supplies: A copy of the Universal Declaration of Human Rights (following two pages) for everyone; yarn; tape; a stack of back issues of your daily newspaper; markers, a few pairs of scissors to share.

Although the Universal Declaration of Human Rights (or UDHR) is not specifically addressed in this session, the violation of these basic rights is the underlying catalyst for most of the nonviolent actions that we are studying.

Everyone should have a copy of the UDHR and a couple of daily newspapers. Allow a few minutes to read over the UDHR and become familiar with it. Then, go through the newspapers looking for articles (or ads) that show:

A right being exercised (mark with a plus + and the number of the UDHR article)

A right being violated (mark with a minus – and the number of the UDHRarticle)

Give about 10 minutes to scan the newspapers. This works best as a group process: encourage everyone to talk it out amongst themselves.

Tape a copy of the UDHR to the wall. At the end of 10-15 minutes (be alert to when concentration begins to flag) have people briefly volunteer to describe the rights they found in the news. Have them tape their article to the wall and connect it to the corresponding article with the yarn. Don't be constrained by the newspapers: if someone knows of a right being exercised or violated, write it on a piece of paper and add it to the display.

If you can leave the display on the wall, invite everyone to take their copy of the UDHR home and bring to the next session any additional articles they may have come across to add to the chart.

Time saver: Give everyone their copy of the UDHR the week before and ask them to look for articles on their own in the intervening week and bring them to this class. You might want to provide some hints. Suggest that the positive exercise of rights can be found in a lot of places: an ad for a movie demonstrates Article #27; a wedding announcement #17. Violations of rights are more apt to be found in the news. During this session have people put their articles on the wall, as described above.

The text that we have provided for the UDHR is an abbreviated, plain text version. The full version can be found at <www.undhr.org>.

Universal Declaration of Human Rights

Whereas recognition of the inherent dignity and of the equal and inalienable rights of all members of the human family is the foundation of freedom, justice and peace in the world,

Whereas disregard and contempt for human rights have resulted in barbarous acts which have outraged the conscience of mankind, and the advent of a world in which human beings shall enjoy freedom of speech and belief and freedom from fear and want has been proclaimed as the highest aspiration of the common people,

Whereas it is essential, if man is not to be compelled to have recourse, as a last resort, to rebellion against tyranny and oppression, that human rights should be protected by the rule of law,

Whereas it is essential to promote the development of friendly relations between nations,

Whereas the peoples of the United Nations have in the Charter reaffirmed their faith in fundamental human rights, in the dignity and worth of the human person and in the equal rights of men and women and have determined to promote social progress and better standards of life in larger freedom,

Whereas Member States have pledged themselves to achieve, in cooperation with the United Nations, the promotion of universal respect for and observance of human rights and fundamental freedoms,

Whereas a common understanding of these rights and freedoms is of the greatest importance for the full realization of this pledge,

Now, therefore, The General Assembly, Proclaims this Universal Declaration of Human Rights as a common standard of achievement for all peoples and all nations, to the end that every individual and every organ of society, keeping this Declaration constantly in mind, shall strive by teaching and education to promote respect for these rights and freedoms and by progressive measures, national and international, to secure their universal and effective recognition and observance, both among the peoples of Member States themselves and among the peoples of territories under their jurisdiction.

ARTICLES:

1 When children are born, they are free and each should be treated in the same way. They have reason and conscience and should act towards one another in a friendly manner.

2 Everyone can claim the following rights, despite: a different sex; a different skin colour; speaking a different language; thinking different things; believing in another religion; owning more or less; being born in another social group; coming from another country. It also makes no difference whether the country you live in is independent or not.

3 You have the right to live, and to live in freedom and safety.

4 Nobody has the right to treat you as his her slave and you should not make anyone your slave.

5 Nobody has the right to torture you.

6 You should be legally protected in the same way everywhere, and like everyone else.

7 The law is the same for everyone; it should be applied in the same way to all.

8 You should be able to ask for legal help when the rights your country grants you are not respected.

9 Nobody has the right to put you in prison, to keep you there, or to send you away from your country unjustly, or without good reason.

10 If you go on trial this should be done in public. The people who try you should not let themselves be influenced by others.

11 You should be considered innocent until it can be proved that you are guilty. If you are accused of a crime, you should always have the right to defend yourself. Nobody has the right to condemn you and punish you for something you have not done.

12 You have the right to ask to be protected if someone tries to harm your good name, enter your house, open your letters, or bother you or your family without a good reason.

13 You should be considered innocent until it can be proved that you are guilty. If you are accused of a crime, you should always have the right to defend yourself. Nobody has the right to condemn you and punish you for something you have not done.

14 If someone hurts you, you have the right to go to another country and ask it to protect you. You lose this right if you have killed someone and if you, yourself, do not respect what is written here.

15 You have the right to belong to a country and nobody can prevent you, without a good reason, from belonging to a country if you wish.

16 As soon as person is legally entitled, he or she has the right to marry and have a family. In doing this, neither the colour of your skin, the country you come from nor your region should be impediments. Men and women have the same rights when they are married and also when they are separated. Nobody should force a person to marry. The government of your country should protect your family and its members.

17 You have the right to own things and nobody has the right to take these from you without a good reason.

18 You have the right to profess your religion freely, to change it, and to practice it either on your own or with other people.

19 You have the right to think what you want, to say what you like, and nobody should forbid you from doing so. You should be able to share your ideas also—with people from any other country.

20 You have the right to organize peaceful meetings or to take part in meetings in a peaceful way. It is wrong to force someone to belong to a group.

21 You have the right to take part in your country's political affairs either by belonging to the government yourself or by choosing politicians who have the same ideas as you. Governments should be voted for regularly and voting should be secret. You should get a vote and all votes should be equal. You also have the same right to join the public service as anyone else.

22 The society in which you live should help you to develop and to make the most of all the advantages (culture, work, social welfare) which are offered to you and to all the men and women in your country.

23 You have the right to work, to be free to choose your work, to get a salary which allows you to support your family. If a man and a woman do the same work, they should get the same pay. All people who work have the right to join together to defend their interests.

24 Each work day should not be too long, since everyone has the right to rest and should be able to take regular paid holidays.

25 You have the right to have whatever you need so that you and your family: do not fall ill; go hungry; have clothes and a house; and are helped if you are out of work, if you are ill, if you are old, if your wife or husband is dead, or if you do not earn a living for any other reason you cannot help. The mother who is going is going to have a baby, and her baby should get special help. All children have the same rights, whether or not the mother is married.

26 You have the right to go to school and everyone should go to school. Primary schooling should be free. You should be able to learn a profession or continue your studies as far as you wish. At school, you should be able to develop all your talents and you should be taught to get on with others, whatever their race, religion or the country they come from. Your parents have the right to choose how and what you will be taught at school.

27 You have the right to share in your community's arts and sciences, and any good they do. Your works as an artist, writer, or a scientist should be protected, and you should be able to benefit from them.

28 So that your rights will be respected, there must be an 'order' which can protect them. This 'order' should be local and worldwide.

29 You have duties towards the community within which your personality can only fully develop. The law should guarantee human rights. It should allow everyone to respect others and to be respected.

30 In all parts of the world, no society, no human being, should take it upon her or himself to act in such a way as to destroy the rights which you have just been reading about.

Adopted by UN General Assembly
Resolution 217A (III)
of 10 December 1948

This page is intentionally left blank

"War is God's way of teaching Americans geography." Ernest Bevin

Class of Nonviolence
Lesson 7
Civil Disobedience and the Pity of War

Essays for Lesson Seven

On the Duty of Civil Disobedience by Henry David Thoreau
The Judge and the Bomb by Miles Lord
Patriotism or Peace by Leo Tolstoy
What Would You Do If? by Joan Baez
Pray for Peace but Pay for War by Maurice F. McCrackin
A Vigil for Life While We Celebrate Death by Colman McCarthy

Questions for Lesson Seven

The principle of a "just war" is merely the clever dodge
of a government bent on violence. Explain.

Write an essay entitled "Developing the attitude of a peacemaker."

Write an essay about your feelings and opinions
concerning civil disobedience.
Does going to jail for your disobedience really change anything?

What do you think the concept of "turning the other cheek"
means in the context of resisting violence and / or aggression.

What would you do if America was ever invaded by a hostile force?

Who are the authors for this session?

Henry David Thoreau: (July 12, 1817 – May 6, 1862) was an American author, naturalist, transcendentalist, tax resister, development critic, and philosopher.

Miles Lord: is the former Minnesota Attorney General, US Attorney for Minnesota and Chief Judge of the Federal District Court.

Leo Tolstoy: (September 9 1828 – November 20 1910) was a Russian novelist, writer, essayist, philosopher, Christian anarchist, pacifist, educational reformer, vegetarian and moral thinker.

Joan Baez: (born January 9, 1941) is an American folk singer, songwriter and antiwar activist.

Maurice F. McCrackin: (1905-1998) was a peace activist pastor defrocked but later reinstated by the Presbyterians.

Display/altar

The overarching theme for this session is civil disobedience, covered by four of the six essays. We've also found that by this point people really, really want to specifically talk about war, especially if it was not covered in any depth during previous lessons. A copy of Picasso's "Guernica" (a nice one is online at <www.westpointgradsagainstthewar.org/images/guernica.jpg>) is a powerful statement. Thoreau's essay on civil disobedience is probably the most historically significant reading of this entire class, so be sure to include a photo of Thoreau in your display. Thoreau and McCrackin both talk about war tax resistance, so a flyer (a free 2-pager is at <www.nwtrcc.org/w4.pdf>; include enough for everyone to take one home) is useful.

Films for this Session

Since 1990, tens of thousands of people have made pilgrimages in November to the gates of Ft. Benning, Georgia to call for the closing of the Pentagon's School of the Americas (SOA), now renamed the Western Hemisphere Institute for Security Cooperation. These two short documentaries are available at a reasonable price from <www.soawatch.org>.

> ***Journey to Awareness - Crossing the Line**: In 2006 a group of high school students produced this 30-minute documentary. The film includes footage from the annual protest at the gates of Fort Benning in Georgia, footage from Latin America, interviews with student activists, folk musician Pete Seeger, as well as Guadalupe Chavez and Linda Aguilar, who engaged in nonviolent direct action to close the SOA.

> ***Convictions - Prisoners of Conscience**: This 20-minute documentary focuses on some of the 2000 SOA protesters who collectively have received 80 years of prison time for their nonviolent civil disobedience.

*Contempt of Conscience 14 minutes, 2006. Available from <www.peacetaxseven.com> This concise film covers the case of seven Britons who are taking their case for war tax resistance to the European Court of Human Rights. Neatly summarizes Thoreau's arguments in a contemporary context. (this DVD was produced in England and will run on a computer, not in a DVD player, in our experience.)

*Making Your Claim as a Concientious Objector to War (created for Veterans for Peace by <www.peppersprayproductions.org>) is a 28 minute "how-to" video on how to apply for CO status.

*Why We Fight 99 minutes, 2006. This documentary examines America's policies regarding making war, reviewing past wars to demonstrate that "the Bush doctrine" of pre-emptive strikes is not a new development. This film complements a discussion on just war.

*Faces of the Enemy Based on the book by Sam Keen, this 1987 documentary investigates how individuals and nations dehumanize their enemies. It comes with a supplementary DVD that updates it for the current political situation. Available from <www.newsreel.org>.

There are several films that complement the poetry and art exercises. ***Voices in Wartime** (2005) <www.voicesinwartime.org> is a documentary that uses poetry to move us into the emotion of war. We found the section where the commandant of West Point explains why they teach war poetry to student-officers especially powerful. Simon Schama's ***Power of Art** (2006) <www.pbs.org/wnet/powerofart> focuses on Guernica; a harder-to-find alternative is ***Pablo Picasso's Guernica** (1999), part of the Discovery of Art series produced by <www.kulturvideo.com>.

Exercise: War Films

Time: 1/2 hour, plus homework
Supplies: A way to show VHS or DVD (optional)

Ask everyone to watch two films: one that glorifies or justifies war (The Green Berets, The Alamo, Henry V, Patton, Braveheart, Rambo, Troy, Gladiator etc.) and one anti-war film. Propose this several weeks prior to ensure everone has time to find, watch and re-flect upon their films. Allot some time for discussion: Are all war films anti-war to some extent? What do most people learn about war though film? Is that important?

Some anti-war films: **Dr. Strangelove** (1964); **Apocolypse Now** (1979); **Slaughterhouse Five** (1972), **Good Morning Vietnam** (1987), **M*A*S*H** (1972), **Born on the Fourth of July** (1989); **The Killing Fields** (1984); **Gallipoli** (1981); **The Deer Hunter** (1978); **Coming Home** (1978); **Oh! What a Lovely War** (1969); **All Quiet on the Western Front** (1930; 1979); **Grand Illusion** (1937); **Duck Soup** (1930); **The Mouse That Roared** (1959); **Catch-22** (1970); **Friendly Persuasion** (1956); **Salvador** (1986); **Wag the Dog** (1998); **Die Brücke** (1959); **The Americanization of Emily** (1964). And some lesser-known ones:

The Burmese Harp (1956) A Japansese soldier in WWII, a self-taught lute player, is shocked by the horrors of war and vows to live a life of prayer.

Grave of the Fireflies (*Hotaru no Haka*) (1988) In this animé, two orphaned Japanese children in the aftermath of WWII are forced to try to survive amidst widespread famine and the callous indifference of their countrymen.

How I Won the War (1967) In this absurdist film, World War II British soldiers die one by one, only to be replaced by ghostly World War I-era soldiers; by the film's end the only man still alive is the one who refused to fight.
The Bedsitting Room (1967) by the same director is about Britain after WWIII and is a good companion film.

Johnny Got His Gun (1972) A young American soldier, hit by a shell on the last day of WWI, lies in a hospital bed, a quadruple amputee who has lost his eyes, ears, mouth and nose, tries to communicate his wish that he be put on show in a carnival as a demonstration of the horrors of war.

Joyeaux Noel (2004) On Christmas Eve dur-ing World War I French, German and British soldiers met in a "no-man's-land" to exchange candy and cigarettes, converse, sing and even play soccer.

King of Hearts (1966) A Scottish soldier, sent to a small French town at the end of WWI to disarm a bomb, unknowingly leaves the door to the insane asylum open while being chased by the Germans. The film ends with the question of who is more insane: those in the asylum or the soldiers on the battlefield.

Lord of War (2005) An arms dealer begins to question the nature of his business and whether what he is doing for a living is moral.

A Midnight Clear (1992) Set in 1944 France, an American Intelligence Squad locates a Ger-man platoon wishing to surrender rather than die in Germany's final war offensive.

No Man's Land (2001) Academy Award-win-ning satire of the war in the Balkans is a black comedy grounded in the brutality and horror of war. Stuck in an abandoned trench between en-emy lines, a Serb and a Bosnian play the blame game while a wounded soldier lies helplessly on a land mine.

Paths of Glory (1955) The title is taken from the Thomas Gray poem *Elegy Written in a Country Church-yard*: "The boast of heraldry, the pomp of pow'r, / And all that beauty, all that wealth e'er gave, / Awaits alike th'inevitable hour. / The paths of glory lead but to the grave." Based loosely on the true story of five French soldiers executed for mutiny during World War I.

Film: *The War Prayer

Time: 20 minutes
Supplies: TV, VCR and copy of film

In 1898 Mark Twain wrote a short story called "*The War Prayer*." (A copy is on the peaceCENTER's Web site at <www.salsa.net/peace/warprayer.html>.) Bitterly opposed to the trend towards US imperialism as demonstrated in the Spanish-American War and what the "Philippine Insurrection," Twain tells how a clergy-man lauding the militarist version of the war is confronted by a stranger who offers a new prayer for the men at war. Twain wrote to a friend, "*I don't think the prayer will be published in my time. None but the dead are permitted to tell the truth.*" He was right.

In 1980 PBS ran a series of little-known Twain stories. "*The War Prayer*" was skillfully tacked onto the end of "*The Private History of a Campaign That Failed.*" Over the years we've been able to pick up a couple of used copies: there always seem to be a few for sale (about $15) on Amazon.com or you might be able to find a copy in your public library.

The *War Prayer* episode is about 12 minutes. We like to show this film at the opening of this lesson to initiate a discussion of what our places of worship tell us about war. What do we pray for? What is the underlying message of "God Bless America?"

If you can't find the film, read the story aloud (it's only three pages) and launch your discussion from there. Or, Aaron Shepard wonderfuly simplified and adapted the story for reader's theater. It's available free online at <www.aaronshep.com/rt/RTE05.html>; eight readers are needed and it lasts about 5 minutes.

Reflective Exercise: Civil Disobedience Quotations

Time: 10-15 minutes
Supplies: A quotation (next page) for every person

By now everyone should have an idea of what to do with quotations. Read them slowly and deliberately, with no discussion between. Let the words wash over you. After all of the quotations have been read, offer some time for respectful reflection. What words or ideas do these quotations have in common? (for example, "conscience"; "to do nothing to side with the oppressors".) Would you like to hear any particular quotation again? Close with a moment of reflective silence.

Civil Disobedience Quotations

Dare to do things worthy of imprisonment if you mean to be of consequence.
Juvenal

Never do anything against conscience even if the state demands it.
Albert Einstein

No radical change on the plane of history is possible without crime.
Hermann Keyserling

It is not what a lawyer tells me I may do; but what humanity, reason, and justice tell me I ought to do.
Edmund Burke

As long as the world shall last there will be wrongs, and if no man objected and no man rebelled, those wrongs would last forever. *Clarence Darrow*

When leaders act contrary to conscience, we must act contrary to leaders.
Veterans Fast for Life

If... the machine of government... is of such a nature that it requires you to be the agent of injustice to another, then, I say, break the law.
Henry David Thoreau

Human history begins with man's act of disobedience, which is at the very same time the beginning of his freedom and development of his reason.
Erich Fromm

Each man must for himself alone decide what is right and what is wrong, which course is patriotic and which isn't. You cannot shirk this and be a man. To decide against your conviction is to be an unqualified and excusable traitor, both to yourself and to your country, let men label you as they may.
Mark Twain

Integrity has no need of rules.
Albert Camus

Disobedience, the rarest and most courageous of the virtues, is seldom distinguished from neglect, the laziest and commonest of the vices.
George Bernard Shaw

We should never forget that everything Adolf Hitler did in Germany was "legal" and everything the Hungarian freedom fighters did in Hungary was "illegal" to aid and comfort a Jew in Hitler's Germany. Even so, I am sure that, had I lived in Germany at the time, I would have aided and comforted my Jewish brothers.
Martin Luther King, Jr.

Ordinarily, a person leaving a courtroom with a conviction behind him would wear a somber face. But I left with a smile. I knew that I was a convicted criminal, but I was proud of my crime.
Martin Luther King, Jr.

If you are neutral in situations of injustice, you have chosen the side of the oppressor. If an elephant has its foot on the tail of a mouse and you say that you are neutral, the mouse will not appreciate your neutrality.
Archbishop Desmond Tutu

Every actual state is corrupt. Good men must not obey laws too well.
Ralph Waldo Emerson

It is dangerous to be right in matters on which the established authorities are wrong.
Voltaire

I am free, no matter what rules surround me. If I find them tolerable, I tolerate them; if I find them too obnoxious, I break them. I am free because I know that *I alone* am morally responsible for everything I do.
Robert A. Heinlein

Reflective exercises: War Poetry

Time: 15-20 minutes
Supplies: Copies of poems (following page) for everyone

On the fourth anniversary of the war on Iraq the peaceCENTER joined the Catholic Worker House and about 25 friends at the gazebo right outside the gates of the Alamo to read poems about war. Tourists gathered 'round with solemn intensity. We brought a bucket of free poems and handed them out.

Poetry can evoke deep responses by reaching the heart in a way that facts and figures cannot. On the next page are five poems that can be handed out and used as discussion starters. You might want to announce this exercise the week before and invite people to bring a favorite poem, if they so choose. At our poetry reading a few people wrote and read poems of their own

There are also numerous collections of contemporary anti-war poetry online from which you can make selections or refer to the class:

> **100 Poets against the war**, 100 Poets against the war redux and 100 Poets against the war 3.0 <www.nthposition.com/100poets.php>
> **Poets Against the War** <www.poetsagainstthewar.org>
> **DC Poets Against the War**

Art Project: Paper Cranes

Time: 15 minutes
Supplies: Instructions for each person (page 131); origami paper

Sadako Sasaki was two when Hiroshima was bombed; she later died of leukemia. She tried to fold 1,000 cranes believing she would get well by doing so. People from around the world now send origami cranes to the Hiroshima Peace Park as a symbol and wish for peace. It is Japanese legend that folding 1,000 cranes (*sen-bazuru*) grants the folder a wish. Sadako's story, told in several books, has become an inspiration for people world-wide.

You can get origami paper at most craft supply stores (it is only colored on one side) or you can cut perfectly square pieces of any paper (traditionally between 6" and 8.5" square.)

Give everyone a stack of paper and the instructions Some people are good at this, some are not: the proficient can help the less nimble-fingered. As you fold, think about the children harmed by war.

"My Subject is war, and the pity of war." Wilfred Owen

Soldier's Dream
By Wilfred Owen. WWI

I dreamed kind Jesus fouled the big-gun gears;
And caused a permanent stoppage in all bolts;
And buckled with a smile Mausers and Colts;
And rusted every bayonet with His tears.

And there were no more bombs,
of ours or Theirs,
Not even an old flint-lock, not even a pikel.
But God was vexed,
and gave all power to Michael;
And when I woke he'd seen to our repairs.

They
By Siegfried Sassoon, WWI

The Bishop tells us: 'When the boys come back
'They will not be the same; for they'll have
fought
'In a just cause: they lead the last attack
'On Anti-Christ; their comrades' blood has
bought
'New right to breed an honourable race,
'They have challenged Death
and dared him face to face.'

'We're none of us the same!' the boys reply.
'For George lost both his legs;
and Bill's stone blind;
'Poor Jim's shot through the lungs and like to
die;
'And Bert's gone syphilitic: you'll not find
'A chap who's served that
hasn't found some change.
' And the Bishop said:
'The ways of God are strange!'

At A War Grave
By John Jarmain, WWII

No grave is rich, the dust that herein lies
Beneath this white cross mixing with the sand
Was vital once, with skill of eye and hand
And speed of brain. These will not re-arise
These riches, nor will they be replaced;
They are lost and nothing now, and here is left
Only a worthless corpse of sense bereft,
Symbol of death, and sacrifice and waste.

Self-Destroyers
By Miles Tomalin, Spanish Civil War

Load upon load of bomb and shell
Shakes down the brick and stone and dust,
But what does all this ruin spell
When only brick and stone are crushed?
Beneath your storm of steel the town
Shivers, and sinks slowly down,
And you believe that hearts lie deep
With homes under the rubble heap!
Your loss is greater than your gain;
Men whose homes are here no longer
Spread the fever of their anger
Through the length and breadth of Spain.
A million hearts you have made stronger,
You have armed a million men.
What you destroy, shatter burn,
Are not the things that in their turn
Will strike you and your cannons dumb,
Is not the spirit in whose name
We built an army, and defied
Your steel, your thunder and your flame:
These cannot die till we have died.
You understand so little. You
Have more than walls to batter through -
Men
Such as your brutish heroes never knew
the way to overcome.

Grass
By Carl Sandburg, WWI

Pile the bodies high at Austerlitz and Waterloo.
Shovel them under and let me work—
        I am the grass; I cover all.

And pile them high at Gettysburg
And pile them high at Ypres and Verdun.
Shovel them under and let me work.
Two years, ten years, and passengers ask the
conductor:
        What place is this?
        Where are we now?

        I am the grass.
        Let me work.

How to Fold a Paper Crane

1

Fold a perfectly square piece of paper in half lengthwise.

2

Make a crease down the middle to mark the center, then diagonally fold down the right side of the paper toward the front.

3

Diagonally fold the left side toward the back.

4

Open the bottom by inserting your finger and fold the left & right points together, spreading the back and front creases.

5

Crease front left and right edges to the center, then back out and pull up bnottom point to produce the shape shown in the next picture.

6

Turn over and do the same for the other side.

7

Fold left and right edges along the dotted line into the center on both the front and back sides..

8

Open both sides along the vertical center axis and crease, producing the split top as shown in #9.

9

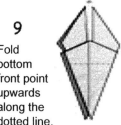

Fold bottom front point upwards along the dotted line.

10

Fold the same point forward and down along the dotted line.

11

Fold bottom point to the back along the dotted line to make a tail.

12

Open lkeft and right sides and crease.

13

Fold down the wings and gently pull on head and tail to expand the body.

14

To complete your paper crane, blow gently into the bottom to help expand the body.

Sadako Sasaki was two when Hiroshima was bombed. She later died of Leukemia. Sadako tried to fold 1,000 cranes, believing she would get well by doing so. People from around the world now send origami cranes to the Hiroshima Peace Park as a symbol and wish for peace.

It is Japanese legend that folding 1000 cranes (senbazuru) grants the folder a wish. Sadako's story, told in several books, has become an inspiration for people world-wide.

Exercise: Sing it, Joan!

Time: 15-20 minutes
Supplies: Boom box(es); lyric sheets (following page)

We admit to going overboard in introducing the music of the peace movement. The high point (or the depths of our dysfunction) was eighteen songs, nine boom boxes and 28 college students. Imagine that!

We recommend something a little more modest. The fourth essay in this session is *"What Would You Do If?"* by Joan Baez, making a perfect opening to enjoy both Joan's clear soprano and some songs about peace and justice.

Quite a few of her songs are available for download from iTunes <www.itunes.com> for 99¢ each; they can be saved to a CD and played on a boom box. Here are some that fit in:

Ballad of Sacco and Vanzetti
Birmingham Sunday
Blessed Are
Blowin' In the Wind
Deportee (Plane Wreck at Los Gatos)
Dona, Dona
Guantanamera
Heaven Help Us All

Imagine
Johnny I Hardly Knew Ye
Joe Hill
Kumbayah
Last Night I Had the Strangest Dream
There but for Fortune
Where Have All the Flowers Gone?
With God On Our Side

We've included the lyrics to *Dona, Dona* (written in Yiddish in 1940 by Aaron Zeitlin and Sholem Secunda); Last *Night I Had the Strangest Dream (*written in 1950 by Ed Mc-Curdy*)* and *Blowin' In The Wind* (written in 1962 by Bob Dylan) on the next page. If you prefer to use different songs, you can find the lyrics by searching on the Internet for *name of song* lyrics.

These songs can be listened to and discussed as a group or, if you can swing it logistically, the conversation will go deeper if you can divide the group into three, furnish each with the music and a boom box, and have them discuss their one song and present their insights to the group.

Some questions we have found useful in relating music to the readings:
What is the TONE of the song? (Is it angry, hopeful, funny, depressing, etc.)
Is there a line or verse that struck a chord with you? Why?
What do you think the songwriter was trying to say?
What was going on in the world when this song was written? Does it still mean the same thing? Does it make sense today?
Do you agree with the message of this song? Why or why not?
Does the song recall anything from the readings for this session?

Dona, Dona

On a wagon bound for market
There's a calf with a mournful eye.
High above him there's a swallow,
winging swiftly through the sky.

Chorus:
How the winds are laughing,
they laugh with all their might.
Laugh and laugh the whole day through,
and half the summer's night.
Dona, Dona, Dona, Dona;
Dona, Dona, Dona, Don.
Dona, Dona, Dona,
Dona; Dona, Dona, Dona, Don.

"Stop complaining!" said the farmer,
"Who told you a calf to be?
Why don't you have wings to fly with,
like the swallow so proud and free?"

Chorus

Calves are easily bound and slaughtered,
never knowing the reason why.
But whoever treasures freedom,
like the swallow has learned to fly.

Chorus

Last Night I Had
the Strangest Dream

Last night I had the strangest dream
I'd ever dreamed before
I dreamed the world had all agreed
To put an end to war

I dreamed I saw a mighty room
Filled with women and men
And the paper they were signing said
They'd never fight again

And when the paper was all signed
And a million copies made
They all joined hands
and bowed their heads
And grateful pray'rs were prayed

And the people in the streets below
Were dancing 'round and 'round
While swords and guns and uniforms
Were scattered on the ground

Last night I had the strangest dream
I'd never dreamed before
I dreamed the world had all agreed
To put an end to war.

Blowin' In The Wind

How many roads must a man walk down
Before you call him a man?
Yes, 'n' how many seas
must a white dove sail
Before she sleeps in the sand?
Yes, 'n' how many times
must the cannon balls fly
Before they're forever banned?
The answer, my friend,
is blowin' in the wind,
The answer is blowin' in the wind.

How many times must a man look up
Before he can see the sky?
Yes, 'n' how many ears
must one man have
Before he can hear people cry?
Yes, 'n' how many deaths
will it take till he knows
That too many people have died?
The answer, my friend,
is blowin' in the wind,
The answer is blowin' in the wind.

How many years can a mountain exist
Before it's washed to the sea?
Yes, 'n' how many years
can some people exist
Before they're allowed to be free?
Yes, 'n' how many times
can a man turn his head,
Pretending he just doesn't see?
The answer, my friend,
is blowin' in the wind,
The answer is blowin' in the wind.

handout for the "Sing It, Joan!" exercise

Exercise/Question: Just War

Time: 15 minutes
Supplies: Just War handout (next page) and chalkboard or big paper

One of the questions Colman McCarthy asks in this section is: "*The principle of a "just war" is merely the clever dodge of a government bent on violence. Explain.*" J**ust War** has a specific meaning and it is beneficial to know it.

Briefly explain to the group that Just War traditionally has two components:
jus ad bellum (the conditions under which it is considered justified to wage war) and ***jus in bello*** (the way in which war is fought "fairly.") (In more recent years, a third category - ***Jus post bellum*** - has been added. It specifies just behavior after war, including peace agreements, reparations, treatment of refugees and the trying of war criminals.)

Write *jus ad bellum* and *jus in bello* in two columns on the board. Spend about five minutes brainstorming examples in each category (Oftentimes people in the class have a hard time coming up with "just" reasons and find it easier to brainstorm "unjust" examples. That's OK. Keep this going until everyone seems to have a good grasp of what the two categories mean.

Hand out the Just War explanation on the next page. Give everyone a few minutes to skim it. Then, repeat Colman's question and continue the discussion in light of a deeper understanding of the concept of Just War.

Some additional questions for consideration:

- Could it be considered a just cause to launch a "pre-emptive strike" in anticipation of attack by another nation?

- In 1974 the United Nations General Assembly defined aggression as "*the use of armed force by a State against the sovereignty, territorial integrity or political independence of another State.*" Would it be considered aggression to enter another country to attack a non-governmental group such as Al-Queda?

- In 2001 Howard Zinn wrote, "*Let's talk about 'military targets. The phrase is so loose that President Truman, after the nuclear bomb obliterated the population of Hiroshima, could say: 'The world will note that the first atomic bomb was dropped on Hiroshima, a military base. That was because we wished in this first attack to avoid, insofar as possible, the killing of civilians.' I suggest that the history of bombing—and no one has bombed more than this nation—is a history of endless atrocities, all calmly explained by deceptive and deadly language like 'accident,' ' military targets,' and 'collateral damage.'*" In modern times, it is possible to distinguish between combatants and noncombatants?

Just War?

Up until the 4th Century, Christians were persecuted in the Roman Empire: many were killed for their beliefs. One thing that angered the Roman government the most was that the Christians were pacifists: they refused to carry weapons or serve in the army. Then, the Emperor Constantine made his empire a Christian-friendly nation. A few years later, when the barbarian hordes were poised to sack Rome, Christians were no longer just a religion — they ran the government and had to decide what to do.

They asked St. Augustine for advice. He turned to the (pagan) philosopher Cicero for inspiration to find a way out of this dilemma. His answer to this question is now called "Just War" and Augustine wrote it down in an essay called *City of God*. It laid the basic outline for most the moral inquiry into just war in the Christian tradition. His proposal was refined by Thomas Aquinas in the 13th century, and is still evolving today.

The Just War tradition has evolved into two concepts: *jus ad bellum* and *jus in bello*. In brief, *jus ad bellum* means that a war is fought for a just cause, while *jus in bello* means that the war is fought in a just way.

Jus ad bellum requires:

1. A war must be a means of last resort. All diplomatic, economic, and political means must be either exhausted or obviously ineffective.

2. A war be declared by legitimate authority. A nation acting alone with no support from other nations is less likely to be considered just when waging war then a large coalition of countries would be; a president acting without the concurrence of congress would be "less just."

3. A war must have a reasonable chance of success.

4. A military action must be morally justifiable. This is generally broken down into four scenarios:
   (a) It is a defense against aggression; the opponent is the attacker;
   (b) It is the correction of injustice - when conditions in another country become so desperate that not even the most basic of human rights are being upheld,
   (c) it be waged with an eye toward establishing a more perfect political order - revenge or punishment are not enough - and (d) it be waged with the end of peace in mind.

Jus in bello requires:

1. The proportionality of the use of force in a war. You don't use a shotgun to kill a cockroach.

2. The combatants discriminate between combatants and noncombatants. Innocent, nonmilitary people should never be made the target of attacks.

3. A country is not responsible for unexpected side effects of its military activity as long as the following three conditions are met:
   (a) The action must carry the intention to produce good consequences
   (b) The bad effects were not intended
   (c) The good of the war must outweigh the damage done by it.

In the just war tradition, there is an implicit injunction against war: an attitude that although war may be at times a necessary evil, it is evil even when necessary.

Deeper into the Question: Just Peacemaking
Time: 15 minutes to infinite
Supplies: None

One of Colman McCarthy's questions for this lesson is: *"What would you do if America was ever invaded by a hostile force?"* After September 11, this question took on a more urgent meaning.

One concept we consistently try to convey is that nonviolence is not a last-minute act but rather a never-ending process. Nonviolence doesn't start 10 minutes after an attack, but rather ten years *before*— or ten generations.

Charles E. Collyer and Ira G. Zepp, Jr., in their book "*Nonviolence: Origins and Out-comes*" (Trafford Publishing: 2006) devised the perfect analogy. Quitting smoking, they explain, is "*never seriously suggested as a cure for the person who is already dying of lung cancer. Rather, we understand that quitting, done early enough, can reduce a person's risk of getting lung cancer in the first place. We would not test the value of quitting smoking by its failure to cure a terminally ill person. Yet, nonviolence is often put to such a test, as a form of eleventh-hour crisis intervention.*" Our sentiments exactly!

Another source we consult to answer this question is Glenn Stassen's **Just Peacemaking: Ten Practices for Abolishing War** *(Pilgrim Press: 1998.)* The underlying thesis of the book is that the Just War tradition has 1,600+ years of development behind it but no one has devoted equal resources establishing what it would mean to work towards a just peace. When the Just War tradition demands, *"A war must be a means of last resort. All diplomatic, economic, and political means must be either exhausted or obviously ineffective,"* What **exactly** does that mean? These are the ten criteria that Stassen and the other authors of this compelling book suggest. This is the answer to the implied second half of the question: the things that could and should have been done ten years before.

1. Support nonviolent direct action.
2. Take independent initiatives to reduce threat.
3. Use cooperative conflict resolution.
4. Acknowledge responsibility for conflict and injustice and seek repentance and forgiveness.
5. Advance democracy, human rights & religious liberty.
6. Foster just and sustainable economic development.
7. Work with emerging cooperative forces in the international system.
8. Strengthen the United Nations and international efforts for cooperation and human rights.
9. Reduce offensive weapons and weapons trade.
10. Encourage grassroots peacemaking groups and voluntary associations.

Exercise: Flag Washing Ceremony

Time: a half hour to an hour
Supplies: gentle soap (such as Woolite); an old-fashioned washtub and scrubbing board; an outdoor clothesline; water

We've never actually done this during a Class of Nonviolence — it's a ceremony that the peaceCENTER traditionally hosts on Flag Day, June 14. After the flags are washed we serve apple pie and lemonade: a traditional all-American party for those who love their country yet mourn its misdeeds. It does, however, complement Tolstoy's essay on peace and patriotism and could be worked into this lesson.

We borrowed this idea from an ad-hoc group in Washington, DC, who hosted their first flag washing in 1991. They have a designated group of washers, each of whom ceremonially washes one stripe of the flag to rid it of stains that soil the purity of our national ideals. They identify the stains as: Blind Patriotism; Classism; Consumerism; Government and Corporate Corruption; Deception; Hypocrisy; Environmental Injustice; Imperialism; Militarism/Occupation; Racism; Sexism; Criminal Injustice and Arrogance.

Ours is less formal. We invite people to bring their own flags and make sure to have one of our own that everyone can use. We invite people to the wash tub to wash a stain of their own definition. We have heard some amazing stories: one weeping man brought the flag that had draped his brother's coffin when his body was returned from the Vietnam War; it had been shoved in a corner of his closet for decades. He washed out the stain of war.

People scrub and talk and weep and shout. They tell of their love of their country, their love of justice and their hope that someday the two may be reconciled. The warm suds are as comforting as a baby's bath. The water heals, cleanses, restores.

This might be a ceremony to hold during the last half hour of the session so that people can invite friends and family to attend. That would also give you more flexibility in extending the time allocated for this exercise / ceremony.

It's also something that you should discuss with the class the week before and obtain a consensus about conducting such a ceremony. This moves across the shadowy border from discussion into activism and should not be attempted if people feel uncomfortable with that transition. That discussion itself can be enlightening.

Going Deeper: Questions About Civil Disobedience

Time: 15 minutes
Supplies: None

Colman McCarthy's second question for this session is: "*Write an essay about your feelings and opinions concerning civil disobedience. Does going to jail for your disobedience really change anything?*" Our community students of nonviolence are not essay writers, so this is something we discuss rather than write about.

Peter Suber, a philosophy professor at Earlham College, raises four hypothetical objections to the use of Civil Disobedience that can be used as a springboard to deeper understanding. (His insightful replies to these objections are online at <www.earlham. edu/~peters/writing/civ-dis.htm>. Feel free to share this with the whole class.) If your group is large, it can deepen discussion to divide into smaller groups, each discussing and reporting back on one question.

Objection: Civil disobedience cannot be justified in a democracy. Unjust laws made by a democratic legislature can be changed by a democratic legislature. The existence of lawful channels of change makes civil disobedience unnecessary.

Objection: Even if civil disobedience is sometimes justified in a democracy, activists must first exhaust the legal channels of change and turn to disobedience only as a last resort.

Objection: We must obey the law under a contract with other members of our society. We have tacitly consented to the laws by residing in the state and enjoying its benefits.

Objection: What if everybody did it? Civil disobedience fails. Most critics prefer to press this objection as a slippery slope argument; the objection then has descriptive and normative versions. In the descriptive version, one predicts that the example of disobedients will be imitated, increasing lawlessness and tending toward anarchy. In the normative version, one notes that if disobedience is *justified* for one group whose moral beliefs condemn the law, then it is justified for any group similarly situated, which is a recipe for anarchy.

Exercise: The Night Thoreau Spent in Jail

Time: 15 minutes
Supplies: Copy of the script (following page) for two actors

If your group enjoys reading out loud (or, better yet, if you have a couple of actors in the group) consider doing a dramatic reading of parts of "*The Night Thoreau Spent in Jail.*" This 1970 play by Jerome Lawrence and Robert E. Lee deals with Thoreau's refusal to pay the poll tax in 1845 and the night he spent in jail because of this act of civil disobedience.

You will need two actors. Thoreau (Henry) at the time of the action was 29 and is youthful, enthusiastic. Emerson (Waldo) is only nine years older, but is stodgy, a little pompous. The Henry Williams referred to in the script was a fugitive slave.

More Thoreau

The excerpt of "On Civil Disobedience" included in this class is abridged; the full essay is available at <thoreau.eserver.org/civil1.html>. A *free* audio book (MP3 format) is available for download or online listening at <www.ejunto.com/thoreau.html>. It comes in two parts and is almost an hour long. The part reproduced in the class manual is the first 8 minutes.

Reminder: Budget Priorities Game

If you didn't conduct the Budget Priorities exercise during Lesson Four (pages 83-85) now would be an excellent time to do it, as it is a perfect complement to a discussion on war tax resistance, which figures heavily in this lesson.

The Night Thoreau Spent in Jail

By Jerome Lawrence and Robert E. Lee, 1970, excerpted from Act 2

HENRY Can you lie in bed every morning? Have your breakfast brought to you – your soft-boiled egg, your toast and tea? Can you lift your right hand to your mouth while your left hand – which is also you – your government – is killing men in Mexico? How can you swallow, Waldo? How can you taste? How can you breathe? You cast your ballot with your right hand – but has your left hand killed Henry Williams, running to be free?

WALDO Because I don't rant like Jeremiah, do you think I'm not outraged? I do what *can* be done!

HENRY That's not enough. Do the impossible. That's what you tell people in your lectures. But you don't really believe any of it, do you? You trundle up and down New England, stepping to the lectern with that beneficent smile, accepting the handshake of mayors and the polite applause of little old ladies. You go on singing your spineless benedictions.

WALDO What I say is not spineless!

HENRY Well, occasionally you've sounded a battle-cry. But you – you yourself – refuse to hear it.

WALDO You are a very difficult man!

HENRY Good. The world is too full of *easy* men.

WALDO Do you want me to go out and advocate violence and rebellion?

HENRY I ask you to stop violence. As for rebellion, do you think this country was hatched from a soft-boiled egg? (*gesturing*) Look around Concord: what do you see? We have become everything we protested against!

WALDO And what are you doing about it, young man? You pull the woods up over your head. You resign from the human race. Could your woodchucks, with all their wisdom, have saved Henry Williams? Are your fish going to build roads, teach school, put out fires? Oh, it's very simple for a hermit to sit off at a distance and proclaim exactly how things could be. But what if everyone did that? Where would we be?

HENRY Where are we, Waldo?

WALDO We are at war. I am aware of it.

HENRY Are you aware of the reasons – slave-holders grasping for more slave territory? *More* slavery and less freedom, is that what you want?

WALDO Henry, we must work within the framework of our laws. The end to this war – the condition of the blacks – this is the business of the President. And the Congress.

HENRY Do you really believe that? Then I guess I'm wrong. I though you had the same disgust that I have for what the military is doing. But if it doesn't trouble you, then I've made a mistake. (with acid sarcasm) You're right to keep still. I'll go back to my woods – and leave you at peace with your war.

WALDO All right, my young conscience. What should I do?

HENRY Declare yourself!

WALDO I will. Absolutely. The next time the occasion arises –

HENRY NOW! A year ago was too late. I'll get you an audience. This afternoon, at Concord Square.

Reflection: The Art of War

Time: 15 minutes

Supplies: a copy of the art (next page) to pass around, or the slide show, available at <www.salsa.net/peace/ebooks/artofwar.html> A description of the art follows the pictures.

For most of history, art glorified war, celebrated victories, lionized generals and served empires. There were exceptions: Jacques Callot's "**the Miseries and Misfortunes of War**" (1633) shows French soldiers pillaging and burning his native Lorraine before being executed by their superiors, lynched by peasants, or surviving to live as crippled beggars. His etchings influenced Goya's horrific "**Disasters of War,**" published in 1863, 35 years after his death.

In the mid-19th century artists began turning away from the aristocratic and state patronage system. In World War I anti-war art (and poetry) flourished, fueled by mass conscription, the scale of the slaughter, the horror of the trenches, the radicalization of ordinary soldiers and the many technological advances that made mass distribution possible.

The art has more impact in a larger size. Web addresses are included along with the brief descriptions. If you have easy access to a projector, they can be shown as a slide show as part of a meditation.

Include them in this lesson's display. Talk about them. Weep over them, find others that speak to you. Paint your own.

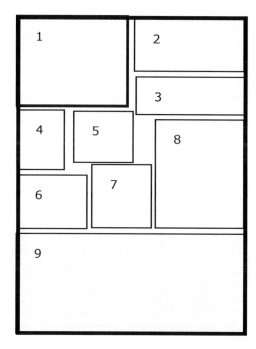

Art is on page 140

Numbers are keyed to the descriptions on page 141

The Art of War

The Art of War
(see key on page 139)

1. **'The Third of May 1808'**, perhaps the first unflinchingly anti-war painting in Western Art, is Goya's response to a tragedy in which Spanish civilians were deliberately killed by Napoleon's troops. <www.wga.hu/html/g/goya/7/714goya.html>

2. Albin Egger-Linz's **'Those Who Have Lost Their Names, 1914'**, shows that war condemns each man to the anonymity of a shared and invisible death. The faces are expressionless or turned towards the ground. The postures are identical. The name-less men have lost all individuality, and sink together in step into the pockmarked earth in which they are to be buried. <www.minerva.unito.it/Theatrum%20Chemicum/Pace&Guerra/Arte/Immagini/Egger-Linz/Egger-LinzDenNamenlosen.jpg>

3. John Singer Sergeant's **'Gassed'** shows the aftermath of a mustard gas attack on the Western Front during World War One. The sun is setting on a society that allows its youth to be wasted in a cruel war. <graphics.jsonline.com/graphics/owlive/img/apr03/gassed041303_big.jpg>

4. Early Dadaist works were random images and textual fragments, but John Heartfield exploited its political possibilities and in 1924 produced **'After ten years: fathers and sons'** showing General Von Hindenburg, a key figure of the First World War and soon to be President of the German Republic, standing in front of skeletons, who are above a marching group of infantry. <www.uic.edu/depts/ahaa/classes/ah111/heartfl1.jpg>

5. In 1942, the year her grandson was killed in action, Kathë Kollwitz created **'Seed Corn Must Not Be Ground,'** her last lithograph. She died in 1945, shortly before the signing of the armistice. <www.humboldt.edu/rwj1/301G/e025.jpg>

6. In Paul Nash's **'We are Making a New World'** the rising sun breaks into No Man's Land on the Western Front. This landscape, constantly reshaped and redrawn by bombardment and attacks is un-mappable, people are excluded, it is ownerless, dead and polluted. The sun will continue to rise each and every day to expose and judge the desecration. <artyzm.com/obrazy/nash_we.jpg>

7. Frans Masereel's **'Dawn'** (1920) reflects fears that a civil war might flare up in the big cities of Germany in the aftermath of World War One. <www.iisg.nl/exhibitions/art/images/maser08.gif>

8. Fritz Eichenberg, who volunteered illustrations for Dorothy Day's *Catholic Worker*, was a German-born artist, printmaker, teacher, Quaker, author, and social activist. This woodcut is **'Child Care Center'** (1980) <www.friendsjournal.org/contents/2002/07july/fritz2.gif>

9. Pablo Picasso's **'Guernica'** was painted for the Spanish Pavilion at the 1937 Paris Exposition in reaction to the Nazi German bombing of civilians in Guernica, Spain during the Spanish Civil War. <www.terra.es/personal/asg00003/picasso/grguer2.jpg>

"I will not eat anything that walks, runs, skips, hops or crawls. God knows that I've crawled on occasion, and I'm glad that no one ate me."
Alex Poulos

Class of Nonviolence
Lesson 8
Animals

Essays for Lesson Eight

Animals, My Brethren by Edgar Kupfer-Koberwitz
Interview on Respect for Animals, with Isaac Bashevis Singer
A Vegetarian Sourcebook by Keith Akers
Diet for a New America by John Robbins
Diet for a Small Planet by Frances Moore Lappé
'Terrorists' for Animal Rights by Colman McCarthy

Questions for Lesson Eight

Read about a contemporary environmental activist. Write about that person.
In what ways was he or she effective in confronting environmental violence?

Do vegetarians carry things too far?
After all, the life of plants is taken to feed them;
what is different from that and taking an animal's life to sustain us?

Do animals have rights? Explain.

How do you envision your relationship with the rest of nature?
Do other elements of Nature exist primarily for our use?
Read the essays of Gary Snyder, *The Practice of the Wild*.

Carson McCullers wrote that,
"before you can love a person you have to start with simpler things
and gradually build your skills - start with a rock, a cloud, a tree."
Is this too simplistic a notion?

True philosophy must start from the most immediate and comprehensive fact of consciousness: 'I am life that wants to live, in the midst of life that wants to live.'   Albert Schweitzer

Who are the authors for this session?

Edgar Kupfer-Koberwitz: was imprisoned in Dachau concentration camp in 1940. His "Dachau Diaries" were published in 1956.

Isaac Bashevis Singer: (1902-1991) was a Nobel Prize-winning Polish-born American writer of both short stories and novels. He wrote in Yiddish.

Keith Akers: is a semi-retired computer programmer who has been active in the vegetarian community, serving at various times as President of the Vegetarian Society of D. C., President of the Vegetarian Society of Colorado, and as an officer in the International Vegetarian Union.

John Robbins: is an American author known for his books on food and health. Born in 1947, he is the son of Baskin-Robbins co-founder Irv Robbins.

Frances Moore Lappé: (born February 10, 1944) is a noted social change and democracy activist, and the author of 15 books, including the three-million-copy bestseller, *Diet for a Small Planet* (originally published in 1971.)

Display/altar

Our peaceCENTER library has a large collection of books that touch on this topic and we typically put some out so that people, as they gather, can look through them. John Robbins' "Diet for a New America" and Frances Moore Lappé's "Diet for a Small Planet," which are extracted in the essays, should be readily available in any public library. A vegan cookbook or two is nice, too.

There are many appropriate art works that you could print and set out. Consider any of the "Peaceable Kingdoms" by the Quaker sign painter Edward Hicks, which are based on a passage from Isaiah 11:6 in the Hebrew Torah: "*The wolf shall also dwell with the lamb, and the leopard shall lie down with the kid; and the calf and the young lion and the fatling together; and a little child shall lead them*." A nice one is at <www.cwrl.utexas.edu/~bump/ranch/peace.jpeg>. (You will notice a group of people in the background of many of Hick's paintings; this is a recreation of William Penn's treaty signing with the Delaware Indians.) A Noah's Ark would also be appropriate. If you want to keep the Edward Hicks thing going, one of his Arks is online at <www.wnd.com/images2/edwardhicksnoahsark.jpg>

Meditation: This Tangerine

Time: about 10 minutes

Supplies: a tangerine (or other similar fruit, such as a Clementine, Satsuma, mandarin orange) and a paper napkin for each person

Start with all sitting silently in your circle, holding your tangerines in both hands before you. The leader guides everyone in a meditation on the tangerine. Adapt this script to make it your own. Everyone else should remain in quiet meditation, invited to offer a respectful reflection at the conclusion.

"As we hold this fruit we hold the sun and the rain that nourished the tree and the fruit. Take a moment to feel the hot sun and the cool rain that we hold in our hands. We hold in our hands the wind and the birds and the bees that pollinated the tree, attracted by the nectar in the fragrant blossoms.

We hold in our hands the farmer who planted the tree and the farm workers who dug the hole and tamped down the soil and kept the orchard free from weeds, who brought in smudge pots when freezes threatened the fruit and watered the tree when it was dry; the farm workers who by the sweat of their labor picked the fruit for us and then moved onto other fields to pick our grapes, our lettuce, our tomatoes.

We hold in our hands the people in the packing plants, who selected the best fruit and put them in boxes. We hold in our hands the truckers and the teamsters and the pilots and ship captains who moved this fruit across the city, the country, the world to bring this fruit to us. We hold in our hands the people who work in the market where we bought this fruit: those who unload the trucks, stock the shelves, ring up our purchase and put it in bags.

Now scrape your nail across the rind of your fruit and smell: can you smell the sunshine and thunderstorms? The winds and the birds? Look at it closely: why is it orange? Why is the skin bitter, and oily? Where did it hang from the tree? Why is it called a tangerine? Where did our fruit come from? California? Florida? Spain, China, North Africa? Could this one be from Tangiers, in Algeria?

Peel your tangerine. Is the skin tough? See the white webbing clinging to the fruit. Pull out a section. How many are there? Does it look like it has seeds? Squeeze out a bit of juice. Smell it. Taste it. Touch it. It is fragrant, sweet, sticky?

Taste a section. Eat it slowly. Can you taste the warmth of the sun and the tang of the rain? The sweat of the farm workers? What does your tangerine taste like? Eat the tangerine."

Films for this Session

*Lisa The Vegetarian
(Seventh Season of The Simpsons, 25 minutes)
This episode has a lot of discussion starters: reasons to become vegetarian; the isolation created when one has values outside the mainstream; cultural pressures; vegetarians being tolerant of others; reconciliation and forgiveness; the importance of community support. If you're not a Simpson's fan this episode may convert you: it's well worth showing in its entirety. You can find this DVD (with all 25 episodes) on Amazon.com for about $35 or it can be rented at many video stores.

*The True Cost of Food (Sierra Club <www.truecostoffood.org> – 15 minutes)
This video can be downloaded from the Web site for showing on a computer (a 7 minute or the full 15 minute version) or you can contact them and they will mail you a DVD (a small donation would be thoughtful.) There is also an 8-page lesson plan available at the same Web site. This video shows the hidden costs in mass-produced food and alternatives that are kinder to the planet and better for us.

The Witness and Peaceable Kingdom are available online from <www.tribeofheart.org>. Both award-winning documentaries are about giving a voice to animals and follow animal activists (in Witness, a Brooklyn man's dormant love for animals was awakened by a kitten and in Peaceable Kingdom the focus is on a cattle rancher turned vegetarian whose controversial appearance on Oprah ended with the talk-show host in court.) The Witness is also available in a Spanish version.

*PETA videos: People for the Ethical Treatment of Animals has a HUGE video archive <www.petatv.com/more.html> that you can download to CD to replay on a computer. Some of the videos are also available for purchase at a reasonable cost. Go through their archive and pick what you want. We've got their four-part series "*Animals Are Not Ours to … experiment on; use for entertainment; eat; wear.*" Each DVD contains many short (4-15 minute) exposés on the specified topic. ($15 each or the whole series for $45 and well worth it!)

Musical Interlude: Don't Slay that Potato

Time: 10 minutes
Supplies: music and player; copy of lyrics for each person (next page)

Melanie Safka's song "*I Don't Eat Animals*" was on her 1970 "Leftover Wine" album, which has recently been re-released (February 2007) by Edsel Records UK (look for it on Amazon.com) If you can't find the recorded music, the song works fine as a poem.

Tom Paxton's humorous song, "*Don't Slay the Potato*" (On his album "*One Million Lawyers and Other Disasters*") directly addresses Colman McCarthy's question, "*Do vegetarians carry things too far? After all, the life of plants is taken to feed them; what is different from that and taking an animal's life to sustain us?*" It has an infectious sing-along chorus.

Either or both of these songs can serve as a fun introduction to this question and lead to a deeper discussion of how we decide what is "edible."

Jainism is an ancient religion, currently with about 10 million adherents, that deeply affected Gandhi: it is from them that he obtained his practice of *ahimsa*. Their dietary practices shed enlightenment on Colman's question. No practicing Jain would eat anything that has five senses, what Westerners would call "meat." They do not eat eggs, considering them the offspring of five-sensed creatures.

They do not eat honey, considering it the excrement of bees; eating excrement is also forbidden. Milk and its by-products (such as butter) are permitted, but it must be "excess" milk, after the calves are fed. The cows must be treated humanely, as if they were members of the family. The most devout of Jains (a monk, for example) will wear a mask over his or her mouth and nose to keep from accidentally snorting a bug. Monks walk barefoot, in a shuffling gait, sweeping a brooms in advance of their footsteps to shoo away any bugs that could be harmed by their footfalls.

Eating root vegetables - don't slay that potato! - is forbidden. One reason is that because they grow underground, small insects and other organisms may be harmed in their harvesting. Another reason is that in pulling up a carrot or onion one destroys the entire plant, while one can harvest a green bean, an apple or a grain of rice without killing the entire plant. Even then, a dried grain or a fruit that drops from the tree is preferred to one harvested before its time. Jains only drink filtered water, partly for health reasons and partly because unfiltered water contains microorganisms.

Jains do not keep pets, as animals are to be left in their natural state, but they are obligated to take in animals that have been hurt or abused. Even rocks are considered to be one-sensed creatures; Jains were the world's first environmentalists, and treat all of the natural world with respect.

Don't Slay That Potato
by Tom Paxton

How can you do it? It's heartless, it's cruel.
It's murder, cold-blooded, it's gross.
To slay a poor vegetable just for your stew
Or to serve with some cheese sauce on toast.
Have you no decency? Have you no shame?
Have you no conscience, you cad,
To rip that poor vegetable out of the earth
Away from its poor mom and dad?

CHORUS:
Oh, no, don't slay that potato!
Let us be merciful, please.
Don't boil it or fry it, don't even freeze-dry it.
Don't slice it or flake it.
For God's sake, don't bake it!
Don't shed the poor blood
Of this poor helpless spud.
That's the worst kind of thing you could do.
Oh, no, don't slay that potato
What never done nothing to you!

Why not try picking on something your size
Instead of some carrot or bean?
The peas are all trembling there in their pod
Just because you're so vicious and mean.
How would you like to
be grabbed by your hair
And ruthlessly yanked from your bed
And have done to you God knows
what horrible things,
To be eaten with full-fiber bread?

(Chorus)

It's no bed of roses, this vegetable life.
You're basically stuck in the mud.
You don't get around much.
You don't see the sights
When you're a carrot or celery or spud.
You're helpless when somebody's
flea-bitten dog
Takes a notion to pause for relief.
Then somebody picks you
and cleans you and eats you
And causes you nothing but grief.

(Chorus)

There ought to be some way
of saving our skins.
They ought to be passing a law.

Just show anybody a cute little lamb
And they'll all stand around and go "Aw!"
Well, potatoes are ugly. Potatoes are plain.
We're wrinkled and lumpy to boot.
But give me a break, kid. Do you mean to say
That you'll eat us because we're not cute?

(Chorus)

I Don't Eat Animals
by Melanie Safka

I was just thinking
about the way it's supposed to be,
I'll eat the plants
and the fruit from the trees,
And I'll live on vegetables
and I'll grow on seeds,
But I don't eat animals
and they don't eat me,
Oh no, I don't eat animals
'cause I love them, you see,
I don't eat animals,
I want nothing dead in me.

I don't eat white flour,
white sugar makes you rot,
Oh, white could be beautiful
but mostly it's not.
A little bit of whole meal,
some raisins and cheese,
But I don't eat animals
and they don't eat me.
Oh no, I don't eat animals '
cause I love them, you see,
I don't eat animals,
I want nothing dead in me.

A little bit of whole meal,
some raisins and cheese,
I'll eat the plants
and the fruit from the trees,
And I'll live on vegetables
and I'll grow on seeds,
But I won't eat animals
and they won't eat me,
Oh no, I'll live on life,
I want nothing dead in me,
You know I'll become life
and my life will become me,
You know I'll live on life
and my life will live on me.

Reflective Exercise: A Voice for Animals

Time: 10-15 minutes
Supplies: A quote (next two pages) on a slip of paper for each person

There are two pages of quotations about animals on the following pages. Cut them up into individual slips (there are 31 of them.)

Hand everyone a quotation or have them draw one from a bowl. Give everyone a minute to read over his or her quotation. Then, have each person stand up and slowly and thoughtfully read their portion out loud to the group. Do this without discussion, one after another.

When all have read, provide a minute or so of reflective silence. Then, ask if anyone would like to have anything repeated, or if they found something especially memorable, confusing, inspiring, profound or meaningful to their lives. Continue the discussion for as long as it is productive.

Exercise: A Vegan Day

Time: 10-15 minutes, plus homework
Supplies: none

The week before, challenge the class to spend a vegan day. This could involve reading packaged food labels; asking servers at restaurants to describe ingredients (and perhaps modify dishes) or coordinating menus with the family's food preparer. It could mean trying a new recipe, a new restaurant or a new grocery store. Ask the class to keep a simple journal so they can report back this week. Did you have to make major changes to the way you eat? Did it affect other people? Were they supportive? Did you run into any surprises about the ingredients in your food? Was the information you needed hard to find? Did you try anything new?

Vegan potluck

Since this is our last session we sometimes celebrate this milestone by sharing a meal together. Have your discussion around the table as you eat.

The week before, ask everyone to bring a vegan dish to share. Make sure everyone understands that a vegan (pronounced VEE-gan; the G is a hard G, like in goose) does not eat any animal products—not even milk, eggs or honey—nor will they wear animal products, including leather, silk or wool. The week's reading explain this in detail. If people need ideas for what to bring, download the peaceCENTER/ Food Not Bombs cookbook from <www.salsa.net/peace/cook1. pdf>, or check out a vegan cookbook from the library. It may help to coordinate food assignments so that you don't get ten tossed salads and nothing else.

A Voice for Animals

Life is life—whether in a cat, or dog or man. There is no difference there between a cat or a man. The idea of difference is a human conception for man's own advantage.
Sri Aurobindo

What is it that should trace the insuperable line? ...The question is not, Can they reason? nor, Can they talk? but, Can they suffer?
Jeremy Bentham

A vegetarian is a person who won't eat anything that can have children.
David Brenner

Man is the only animal that can remain on friendly terms with the victims he intends to eat until he eats them.
Samuel Butler

We don't need to eat anyone who would run, swim, or fly away if he could.
James Cromwell

The time will come when men such as I will look upon the murder of animals as they now look on the murder of men.
Leonardo DaVinci

There is no fundamental difference between man and the higher animals in their mental faculties... The lower animals, like man, manifestly feel pleasure and pain, happiness, and misery.
Charles Darwin

The human commitment to harmony, justice, peace, and love is ironic as long as we continue to support the suffering and shame of the slaughterhouse and its satellite operations.
Karen Davis

You put a baby in a crib with an apple and a rabbit. If it eats the rabbit and plays with the apple, I'll buy you a new car.
Harvey Diamond

We all love animals. Why do we call some "pets" and others "dinner?"
k.d. lang

Love animals: God has given them the rudiments of thought and joy untroubled. Do not trouble their joy, don't harass them, don't deprive them of their happiness, don't work against God's intent. Man, do not pride yourself on superiority to animals; they are without sin, and you, with your greatness, defile the earth by your appearance on it, and leave the traces of your foulness after you - alas, it is true of almost every one of us!
Fyodor Dostoyevsky

At the moment our human world is based on the suffering and destruction of millions of non-humans. To perceive this and to do something to change it in personal and public ways is to undergo a change of perception akin to a religious conversion. Nothing can ever be seen in quite the same way again because once you have admitted the terror and pain of other species you will, unless you resist conversion, be always aware of the endless permutations of suffering that support our society.
Arthur Conan Doyle

Nonviolence leads to the highest ethics, which is the goal of all evolution. Until we stop harming all other living beings, we are still savages.
Thomas Edison

Our task must be to free ourselves . . . by widening our circle of compassion to embrace all living creatures and the whole of nature and its beauty.
Albert Einstein

You have just dined, and however scrupulously the slaughterhouse is concealed in the graceful distance of miles, there is complicity.
Ralph Waldo Emerson

The greatness of a nation and its moral progress can be judged by the way its animals are treated.
Mahatma Gandhi

As long as there are slaughterhouses, there will be battlefields.
Leo Tolstoy

To my mind, the life of a lamb is no less precious than that of a human being.
Mahatma Gandhi

I am in favor of animal rights as well as human rights. That is the way of a whole human being.
Abraham Lincoln

If slaughterhouses had glass walls, everyone would be a vegetarian.
Paul McCartney

Why does Sea World have a seafood restaurant? I'm halfway through my fishburger and I realize, Oh my God. I could be eating a slow learner.
Lynda Montgomery

When it comes to having a central nervous system, and the ability to feel pain, hunger, and thirst, a rat is a pig is a dog is a boy.
Ingrid Newkirk

For as long as men massacre animals, they will kill each other. Indeed, he who sows the seed of murder and pain cannot reap joy and love.
Pythagoras

To a man whose mind is free there is something even more intolerable in the sufferings of animals than in the sufferings of man. For with the latter it is at least admitted that suffering is evil and that the man who causes it is a criminal. But thousands of animals are uselessly butchered every day without a shadow of remorse. If any man were to refer to it, he would be thought ridiculous. And that is the unpardonable crime.
Romain Rolland

If a group of beings from another planet were to land on Earth — beings who considered themselves as superior to you as you feel yourself to be to other animals — would you concede them the rights over you that you assume over other animals?
George Bernard Shaw

While we ourselves are the living graves of murdered beasts, how can we expect any ideal conditions on this earth?
George Bernard Shaw

Humans - who enslave, castrate, experiment on, and fillet other animals - have had an understandable penchant for pretending animals do not feel pain. A sharp distinction between humans and "animals" is essential if we are to bend them to our will, make them work for us, wear them, eat them - without any disquieting tinges of guilt or regret. It is unseemly of us, who often behave so unfeelingly toward other animals, to contend that only humans can suffer. The behavior of other animals renders such pretensions specious. They are just too much like us.
Dr. Carl Sagan & Dr. Ann Druyan

Animals are my friends... and I don't eat my friends.
George Bernard Shaw

In their behavior toward creatures, all men are Nazis. Human beings see oppression vividly when they're the victims. Otherwise they victimize blindly and without a thought.
Isaac Bashevis Singer

Even in the worm that crawls in the earth there glows a divine spark. When you slaughter a creature, you slaughter God.
Isaac Bashevis Singer

I did not become a vegetarian for my health, I did it for the health of the chickens.
Isaac Bashevis Singer

All the arguments to prove man's superiority can not shatter this hard fact: In suffering, the animals are our equals.
Peter Singer

Nothing more strongly arouses our disgust than cannibalism, yet we make the same impression on Buddhists and vegetarians, for we feed on babies, though not our own.
Robert Louis Stevenson

I cannot fish without falling a little in self-respect...always when I have done I feel it would have been better if I had not fished.
Henry David Thoreau

The animals of the world exist for their own reasons. They were not made for humans any more than black people were made for whites or women for men. *Alice Walker*

Wrapping it up

Time: about a half hour
Supplies: None

You can, of course, just stop. Last essay read, last question answered. If you did the "*letter to myself*" exercise in lesson one (page 23) you've returned the letters: handed them back as people arrived and gave everyone a chance to read his or her letter privately and, if they choose, to the group. It's been fun, it's over, so long, it's been good to know 'ya.

It's not enough.

Consider carving some time from this last session to review the material you have covered in the past eight weeks. Some questions that can spark memory:

Did you learn anything that has surprised you?

Is there something in the material we have studied that still niggling at you: something concept you still struggle with, or that bothers you or that you would like to learn more about?

Have you used any of the material we have studied, either by changing how you interact with others or in in your attirude towards world events?

Do we want to continue this conversation about nonviolence? How?

Many groups, or at least some members of the group, *do* want to continue the conversation. If yours does, by now you know each other well enough to have ideas about how best to do this. *We've* found that one of the best way to continue learning is to facilitate the Class of Nonviolence for another group. Other ideas: start a nonviolence book discussion group or get together once a month to watch a film or just share a meal and converse about world affairs.

We'd like to hear from you: Where did you conduct the Class of Nonviolence? How did it go? Who participated? Did any of these exercises work especially well? Were some of them unmitigated disasters? Did you tweak anything to make it work better for your group? Did you add anything new? You can send an e-mail to pcebooks@yahoo.com.

.

Reading List

Had enough? No? Here is an even dozen books to take you deeper into the heart of nonviolence.

Lesson one: If you only get one film, we recommend "**A Force More Powerful,**" available from <www.aforcemorepowerful.org>. It's the perfect film (there is also a companion book by Peter Ackerman and Jack Duvall) for teaching and learning about nonviolent movements. Mark Kurlansky's "**Nonviolence: Twenty-five lessons from the history of a dangerous idea**" is a sweeping summary of the philosophy and history of nonviolence. For those interested in exploring the interplay between inner peace and world peace, we recommend Thich Nhat Hanh's "**Peace is Every Step: The power of mindfulness in everyday life.**"

Lesson two: We find Gandhi's own writing a hard slog, but a gentle and intensely personal introduction is his grandson Arun Gandhi's "**Legacy of Love: my education in the path of nonviolence.**"

Lesson three: The ideal follow-up to this lesson is Day's autobiography, "**The Long Loneliness.**"

Lesson four: Every nonviolent bookshelf should have a well-thumbed copy of "**A Testament of Hope: The Essential Writings and Speeches of Martin Luther King, Jr.**"

Lesson five: It's out of print, but used copies are readily available of "**We Are All Part of One Another: Barbara Deming Reader,**" edited by Jane Meyerding. Deming perfectly captures the intersection between feminism and nonviolent activism.

Lesson six: We recommend a pair of anthologies, "**The Power of Nonviolence: Writings by Advocates of Peace,**" edited by Howard Zinn and "**Peace Is the Way,**" edited by Walter Wink for the Fellowship of Reconciliation.

Lesson seven: A thoughtful counterpoint to the idea of a just war is "**Just Peacemaking: Ten Practices For Abolishing War**" by Glen H. Stassen.

Lesson eight: In "**The Ethics of What We Eat: Why Our Food Choices Matter,**" Peter Singer and Jim Mason document corporate deception, waste and desensitization to inhumane practices by examining three families' grocery buying habits and the motivations behind those choices.

If you can't find these books locally (support your local independent bookseller!) they can be purchased online from <www.salsa.net/peace/amazon>. The peaceCENTER gets a small commission from Amazon.com that we use to buy more books for the Arun and Sunanda Gandhi Peace and Resource Center.

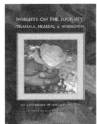

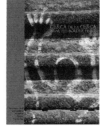

6181501R0

Made in the USA
Lexington, KY
26 July 2010